Silent Stars Speak

In memory of
George A. Katchmer,
author and silent film historian

SILENT STARS SPEAK

Interviews with Twelve Cinema Pioneers

by

Tony Villecco

For
Denis!
A very good
friend and fine
person who has many)
talents of his own.
Write your book.
Tony Villecco
2001

McFarland & Company, Inc., Publishers
Jefferson, North Carolina, and London

Acknowledgments: A book doesn't just write itself, and neither did this one. Many people generously assisted me with encouragement or information, photographs, materials and most important, their time and expertise. Thanks must be extended to Norma Anderson, Bill and Cessie Barbour, Diana Serra Cary, John DeBartolo, Rozella (Renish) Decker, Carrie DeWitt, John Drennon, Virginia Durant, Colleen Hailey at Binghamton University, the late George Katchmer to whom I dedicate this book, Bob King, Nancy Kurisco, Marina Loos, Ron Magliozzi from the Museum of Modern Art Department of Film for his wonderful filmography on Baby Peggy, Randal Malone, Marc McElhatten from the Cinema Department of Binghamton University, Teresa McWilliams, Ken and Merrily Peach, the Max Reinhardt Archive; Special Collections at Binghamton University, the ever supportive Brenda Rhodes, George A. Schoenbrunn, Phil Serling, Lee Shepherd, John Skillin, the late Mary Anne Styburski, Gene Vazzana, and Loretta Young.

I must also express appreciation to the staff at the New York Public Library for the Performing Arts at Lincoln Center and particularly to my secretary, Lynne Biango, for her countless hours transcribing tapes and running around New York City with me. I also credit the wonderful Internet Movie Database for filling in some missing links, and offer thanks to anyone else whose name I have overlooked.

Lastly and most importantly, I thank the twelve wonderful people represented in this book who shared of their time and memories so that the readers might have a clearer sense of "what it was like" then to make a movie and be a star. My gratitude is endless.

Library of Congress Cataloguing-in-Publication Data

Villecco, Tony, 1956–
    Silent stars speak : interviews with twelve cinema pioneers
/ by Tony Villecco.
        p.   cm.   Includes index.
    Contents: Baby Peggy—Priscilla Bonner—Virginia Cherrill—
Pauline Curley—Jean Darling—Douglas Fairbanks, Jr.—
Francis Lederer—Molly O'Day—Anita Page—Charles "Buddy"
Rogers—David Rollins—Andrew Stone.
    ISBN 0-7864-0814-6 (softcover : 50# alkaline paper) ∞
    1. Motion picture actors and actresses—United States—
Interviews.   2. Silent films—United States. I. Title.
PN1998.2.V55   2001   791.43'028'092273—dc21 [B]   00-48995

British Library cataloguing data are available

On the cover: Anita Page, 1928. (*Photograph courtesy of Anita Page*)

*McFarland & Company, Inc., Publishers
  Box 611, Jefferson, North Carolina 28640
   www.mcfarlandpub.com*

Contents

"Cagney made a come-back after a long retirement in RAG-TIME and there was a lot of publicity about that. But Pola topped *all* retirements. She had been out of the limelight for years and now ... here she was, Valentino's silent mourner, back before the public, like SUNSET BOULEVARD. She was *still* big—the *movies* had gotten smaller!"

(Actor Eli Wallach to author on working with silent film
legend Pola Negri in The MOONSPINNERS, 1963)

Introduction

Cinema pioneers—what are they and what sets them apart? The art of the film is so vast that it seems an impossible and unfair task to isolate a "chunk" of time and chisel away at *how* it worked, *why* it worked. Perhaps, then, I am as much infatuated with the decade of the twenties as our progress as a nation and of the world itself.

Certainly no other period of time saw so much change and so swiftly. From economic highs to the crash and burn on Wall Street; a still hustling population of immigrants arriving in America; going to and coming home from war, we were a nation in *motion*. So then it was a natural and inevitable thing to witness a boom in the arts, particularly cinema.

Ballet originated in Europe and Russia, yet dance in all regions took on new shape and importance now. Opera, an Italian pastime, was alive and well in America with the emphasis on the foreign singer, unlike today with so many fine American singers. Theater, too, had thrived, from the small touring companies to the glare of Broadway and the lure of vaudeville. But film was still so new yet changing so very fast.

Who would imagine a film that talked? Or a film in color? Novelty, some said. Even Hollywood wasn't convinced of the importance of this new art form despite the fact it hadn't started in California but ended up forever associated with it. Hence the studios and the beginning of the "star system"—the press, the hype, the bigger-than-life person playing on a screen in your town. So it would be that films would graduate from one reel flickers to feature length pictures with actors becoming household names.

The earliest film represented in this book was made in 1915. The

1

oldest was in 1931, an era of sound yet still a silent film. It was Chaplin's *City Lights*. Hesitant to make the crossover, he undoubtedly found that a silent picture could often tell the story so much more eloquently than one with a soundtrack. It should be of no surprise then to learn that practically all of Chaplin's films survive when so many other silent films were tossed aside or disintegrated.

Baby Peggy enchanted audiences as no other child star had done. Priscilla Bonner could have easily made the transition to sound but chose to leave the profession. Virginia Cherrill was a lovely blonde with no acting ambition, yet is forever remembered as the blind girl. Pauline Curley saw the earliest of Hollywood's scandals. Jean Darling romped with a bunch of kids and made history. Douglas Fairbanks, Jr., lived up to his father's legacy as a true legend. Francis Lederer, one of the most talented and versatile actors, will have lived over a century at the approach of the millennium. Molly O'Day was an Irish lass with a crush on her co-star. Anita Page remembered the very first Academy Awards. Charles "Buddy" Rogers stole America's heart while "America's Sweetheart" would eventually steal his. David Rollins named his car Clara Bow due to its red wheels, like Clara's hair. Director Andrew Stone despised the early makeup in silent films.

These gracious people make up this book. Listen to their stories, hear their voices. They are among those pioneers who laid the groundwork for what was to be, for what *is*.

My goal has been to entertain, but also to educate. If one ever wanted to know what was it like back then to make a movie, I hope it is answered here. Most importantly, enjoy the music in their voices, the dance of their joyful experiences and the theater of their memories by reliving their wonderful careers.

Baby Peggy

It was the fall of 1996 that New York's Museum of Modern Art held a "by invitation only" book signing and screening of new-found films of the former Baby Peggy, Diana Serra Cary. I had spoken to Diana several times on the telephone and interviewed her from her California home.

Her autobiography, *Whatever Happened to Baby Peggy? The Life and Times of Hollywood's Pioneer Child Star* (St. Martins, 1996), had just been published, and MOMA'S Department of Film had scheduled two days of film showings with the star.

Seeing her in person was both exciting and inspiring. She is an elegant woman. Tall, with her dark hair swept up and sporting red lipstick and a chic outfit, it was hard to visualize this striking woman as one of the pioneers in the silent film era. But indeed, she was one of its biggest child stars of the 1920s.

Perhaps more intriguing were her fans that day. From very young people to ladies and gentlemen well into their eighties and beyond, a sense of deep loyalty and great admiration existed among us. I overheard one elderly gentleman telling another, "Yeah, I always liked Baby Peggy more than Shirley Temple. Shirley was too cutesy cutesy but Baby Peggy had *spunk!*"

After the showing of a recently discovered Baby Peggy film, *Sweetie* (1923), thanks to the efforts of film historian John DeBartolo, we were welcomed upstairs to the gift shop where a book signing was held. Wonderfully orchestrated by the head of MOMA'S Film Study Center, Ron Magliozzi, Diana signed book after book, allowing for questions and photos.

5/28/96 To Tony —
warm personal regards,
"Baby Peggy"

(Diana Serra Cary)

With Best Wishes from
Baby Peggy

Baby Peggy in 1922.

What I have included here is one of two interviews we assembled together. Diana talked at length about these early years and what she remembered as one of the biggest "little" stars of that time.

A Very "Grown Up" Child

An adorable portrait of Baby Peggy on a postcard issued in France in the 1920s.

"Everything was new, every day was different. We were pioneering; I didn't know when we started out in the morning what we would be doing that day."

Diana Serra Cary, the former "Baby Peggy," was obviously enjoying reminiscing about her early days in Hollywood. Unquestionably one of the biggest child stars during the silent film era, she understood almost immediately that stardom meant work. (At the height of her career, Baby Peggy was signed for $1 million per film with Century Studio producer Sol Lesser.) But with a career in the large midst of older people, she quickly adapted to the world of adults, and in doing so gave up what any other little girl could look back upon: her childhood.

"I remember specifically being taken to Pickfair [Douglas Fairbanks, Sr., and Mary Pickford's estate] and I remember Mary and Doug. It was a full day there but I considered them workers like me. The fact that they were older didn't impress me because I worked with older people all the time.

"I always liked professional people. If the person was professional on the set, I liked them. If they weren't, I had very little patience with them. That was really my yardstick."

Years later in 1932, Diana was reunited with Fairbanks, who was

Baby Peggy as Mustard Seed in a production of *Midsummer Night's Dream* at Hollywood Bowl to benefit actors, in 1922.

living not in Pickfair but in his large dressing room at United Artists Studio. "When I came back to Hollywood, he was more or less out of films and producing documentaries on Africa, India, safaris and things like that.

"He was very nice to me and at the time, I remember he helped get an article and picture in the paper of the two of us together so that I got a job. I did make several talkies but they were small parts.

"Actually, he was supposedly still married to Mary Pickford but they were living apart. He was living in his dressing room for a very good reason—because they were separated!"

Baby Peggy, circa 1922, making *Whose Baby Are You?* (the title of which was later changed), seen here not in costume.

HOLLYWOOD'S FOUNDING FATHERS

"Hollywood was founded in the 1880s. The founding fathers of Hollywood were strict prohibitionists, or non-drinkers. I remember seeing them as very proper, like the 'American Gothic' painting. They watched from their porches and verandahs as we shot our films on their lawns. They use to call us 'camera Gypsies.'

"These were the original citizens of Hollywood. In those days it was made up of newcomers from Iowa who had come West and had no connection to anything theatrical at all. Mostly retirees, they'd moved out there to enjoy their exotic orange trees in their backyards. They had nothing like that in Iowa.

"They watched us with a certain degree of distaste and disapproval while we made movies on their lawns. And I remember thinking that the wickedest thing they must have ever done was to paint their houses pastel pink and yellow!"

PARTY TOWN

There was plenty of playtime, at least for the adults whom Baby Peggy grew up with and around. Being the "roaring 20s" with plenty of bootleg booze, Hollywood was somewhat like a town gone mad. So much in film was new, and rapid advances were happening almost daily with filmmaking, let alone the world itself which was caught up in continual change.

"Picture people, as they were called, were not wicked like people are wicked today, but they were 'innocently wicked.' Like children being naughty because no one in authority was watching over them.

"They danced and played games like 'Murder,' which was a ridiculous game! It almost killed them! My mother told me years later that she played this game at one Hollywood mansion. They turned off all the lights and then one person was named the victim and another, the murderer. And in the dark, fueled with lots of bootleg booze, they fell into fountains and fell down stairs. It was madness!

"All of Hollywood loved to play. I often thought of them, including my parents, as children while *I* felt *I* was the adult! They were always doing silly things. They danced and drank too much and laughed; they played jokes on each other and just seemed to have so much fun doing silly things! But early Hollywood people never tried to hurt anyone."

THE ADVENT OF SOUND

With "talkies" looming on the horizon, many fine actors would be out of work. It wasn't always the case as with John Gilbert, who was

Baby Peggy as a vamp in *Peg o' the Movies*, 1922 (courtesy of Diana Serra Cary).

laughed off the screen due to the nature of his speaking voice and early sound technology. Early sound, however, was less than desirable, and if it were perfected sooner, perhaps many more actors could have made the transition.

"The early recordings were terrible. You could hardly hear the

DECEMBER 1923   25¢

CLASSIC

COMBINED WITH SHADOWLAND   A BREWSTER PUBLICATION

Baby Peggy on the cover of the December 1923 *Motion Picture Classic* **(courtesy of John Drennon).**

dialogue. The stars who couldn't make it didn't have a prayer in Hollywood. After talkies came in, all that most of these former actors could get was 'extra' work.

"Many of them committed suicide. Every weekend somebody would walk into the ocean or put their head in a gas oven or run the car in a closed garage until they were overcome by carbon monoxide gas.

"It was a tough time in Hollywood after talkies came in. One cause of the trouble was that producers had no respect for silent films as an art form. They did not realize it had valuable qualities quite apart from sound. The medium and the people who had pioneered silents were both the victims of Hollywood's first experience with a 'throw away society.'

"They made no attempt to salvage anything or *anyone*, from the wreckage. It was a social phenomena."

LOSS AND DESTRUCTION OF FILMS

Baby Peggy also remembers terrible loss and destruction of films. Luckily, several of her own films were later salvaged and carefully reconstructed. For some, however, the loss continues to be a permanent one.

"Films like my own, for example, and many others, were shown around the world in the silent era. All that exhibitors had to do in Czechoslovakia, Russia or China, was to translate English titles into the local language. So these films circled the globe very rapidly.

"But then they were supposed to be sent back to the studios from which they came. And that was when my producers melted them down to retrieve the two dollars and fifty cents worth of silver nitrate in the film! This was common practice in Hollywood.

"Many of these European exhibitors overseas who considered film an art form were good people who simply kept their copies. They didn't send them back because they knew what happened when they did. They were kept in vaults and cared for by film experts in such countries as France, Czechoslovakia, Austria and England. They husbanded these films for the rest of us.

"But Hollywood did not. They'd gotten their money out of them, you see. They invested maybe five thousand dollars in a Baby Peggy comedy and after the film had circled the globe, it earned about a half million dollars! *And* the five thousand investment included my *salary* in those early days!

"One other thing that happened at Century Studio where my comedies were made, was a night fire in 1926. It burned to the ground and what films that were left in the vault were all destroyed. [Nitrate

The author with Diana Serra Cary (Baby Peggy) at her book signing at the Museum of Modern Art, New York, fall 1996.

stock films were known to be highly flammable and could literally "burst" into flames, destroying the reels.]

"Especially after talkies came in, nobody collected silent film or silent film stars' portrait stills and autographs. I saw *thousands* of stills being burned in Hollywood's backyard incinerators where homeowners burned their trash. I also saw other films that had turned to dust and jelly in the can because nobody cared or knew how to preserve them."

An interesting article appeared in the August 1917 issue of *Dramatic Mirror* which specifically tells how, during World War I, film stock was in demand by the Germans for its potentially high explosive composition. "Government officials … have requested every representative motion picture producer and distributor in the country to refrain from selling mutilated motion picture films to any person, whatsoever, until after the termination of the war.

"The basis for motion picture films is gun cotton, which is also the basis of nearly every high explosive. It is understood that Germany and her allies are experiencing a shortage in gun cotton to such an extent that they are prepared to pay fabulous sums for any substance of which gun cotton is a component part."

Within the Law (1917) was one of the films retrieved after an investigation occurred and revealed that "the Greater Vitagraph masterpieces had been stolen in order that they might be sold to representatives of the enemies of the entente allies…. [A]gents of Germany have been busy for several months in an effort to purchase the tremendous supplies of disused motion picture film held in storage by the large distributing companies."

This is a devastating thought when one thinks of the countless lost, stolen or decaying films that will never be seen again. That a war effort could have brought this to light is even more intriguing, and film preservationists the world over must be recoiling in horror.

The article concludes that "as soon as a motion picture film producing or distributing company receives a report from an exhibitor or from a branch office that a print of a picture has been damaged, the print is called in, 'junked' and placed in storage. There are many millions of feet of damaged film in storage. In one western city, it is declared, that there is an entire warehouse given over to the storage of damaged films. The secret agents of Germany [are] offering as high as forty-two cents a pound for it, as against the usual market price of about eighteen cents a pound."

Who is to say which of those damaged films would have been candidates for film restoration? The thought is indeed a most sad and tragic one.

GLIMMER OF HOPE

"Men like the late John Hampton in Hollywood deserve tremendous credit for saving many, many films, among them my own. He founded the Silent Movie Theatre in Hollywood and he did a reconstruction on my *Captain January* [1924], *The Family Secret* [1924] and *Helen's Babies* [1925]. I don't know where John got his two copies of the original *Captain January*, but he spliced them and made them into a complete reconstructed film.

"I know there is an incomplete copy of *Helen's Babies* in Russia, but there's a complete copy of John Hampton's film. [The author has seen the restored print of this film at the Syracuse Cinefest. "Baby Peggy" continues to hold her appeal to present day audiences.]

"It is to these people who worked to salvage film that I've dedicated my autobiography. If it hadn't been for these dedicated souls, there wouldn't be anything left at all.

"Jackie Coogan's *Oliver Twist* [1922] was deliberately destroyed by its producer for the silver nitrate, but a rare print was discovered in Czechoslovakia in the late seventies and he helped to restore the English titles. Blanche Sweet also had several of her films saved in this way. The original *Anna Christie*, which she made in 1923 or '24, was found decades later in Czechoslovakia."

Diana Serra Cary still maintains a healthy and positive attitude in spite of her early exposure to the "adult" world in which she wasn't allowed to have a childhood. She is an acclaimed and respected author on early Hollywood and remains a strong advocate for the preservation and restoration of lost films.

"I believe you're dealt a hand and you do the best you can. There's always good in it and there's always bad. You try to find more of the good and forget the negatives."

FILMOGRAPHY*

Century Comedies

Century Film Corporation. Released by Universal. 2 reels.

Executive producers Julius and Abe Stern; production manager Sig Neufeld; executive secretary Zion Myers; animal trainers Charles Gay and Peter Morrison; chief electrician D. C. Stegal; assistant electricians Charles Gould, Walter Gould and Harold Story; directors included J. G. Blystone, Tom Buckingham, James Davis, Harry Edwards, Fred C. Fishback, Arvid Gillstrom, Alf Goulding, Albert Herman, Fred Hibbard, Vin Moore, Zion Myers, Herman C. Raymaker, Chuck Reisner, David Smith, Noel Smith, Bert Sternbach, William H. Watson.

The Century Film Corp. was founded in 1917 to produce comedies starring Alice Howell. By 1920 the studio was best known for its animal comedies featuring the Century lion, "wonder" dogs, and mule and trick horses. Century followed a strict "unit" system for the production of shorts. Each "unit" was built around a star comedian, such as Brownie the dog, and consisted of a self-contained production crew headed by a director

who also acted as unit producer and scriptwriter. So crucial was the unit director to the creation of individual films at Century, and so small and overworked was the studio's directorial staff, that a director's disability during production could mean the cancellation or longterm shelving of a film. After a number of unbilled performances as the studio's "baby" and as a sidekick for the Century dog stars Brownie and Teddy, Baby Peggy was made the star of her own "unit" in mid–1921. Directors Alf Goulding and Arvid Gillstrom were responsible for most of the official Baby Peggy productions. Personnel for the "Baby Peggy unit" included, at various times, assistant producer David Smith; chief cameraman Jerry Ash; assistant cameraman Roy Eslick; editor and title writer Joe W. Farnham; art director Tom O'Neil; property manager Chuck Harris; extra and production assistant Johnny Belasco; director of publicity Mrs. Maud Robinson Toombs; and actors Max Asher, Joe Bonner, Jack Earle, Inez McDonnell, Fred Spencer, and Blanche Payson.

A number of the Baby Peggy films were premiered in advance of

---

The author is indebted to Ronald S. Magliozzi, the head of The Museum of Modern Art Film Study Center, for this filmography. Mr. Magliozzi has done extensive research on Baby Peggy's films and it is largely to his credit, that several of her earlier films have been located and restored. They will now be preserved for future generations to enjoy and to study as well. He was responsible for not only assembling a screening of her rare "re-discovered" shorts at MOMA along with her book signing, it was Ron whose extensive filmography appears in her book and he graciously allowed me to reprint it here as well. This is certainly not to minimize the importance of the other players represented here but moreover, to include a guide to Baby Peggy's film work which was previously not compiled and documented.

their national release at important theaters in New York and Los Angeles, as a means of enhancing their prestige and generating reviews which were later used to promote the films when they went into general release. Although this was a common practice among producers of short films at this time, Century president Julius Stern claimed it as a uniquely successful element in the studio's exploitation of its product.

ETR = Exhibitors Trade Review
MPN = Motion Picture News
MPW = Moving Picture World

Her Circus Man—March 9, 1921. Directed by James Davis.
On with the Show—April 20, 1921. Directed by James Davis.
The Kid's Pal—April 27, 1921. Directed by Tom Buckingham. *Cast:* Brownie the dog, Florence Lee, Bud Jamison, Billy Engle. *Review:* MPW, March 19, 1921.
Playmates—May 18, 1921. Directed by Fred C. Fishback. *Cast:* Brownie the dog.
On Account—June 8, 1921. Directed by William H. Watson.
Pals—June 15, 1921. Directed by Tom Buckingham. *Cast:* Brownie the dog. *Review:* MPW, May 14, 1921.
Third Class Male—July 20, 1921. Directed by William H. Watson. *Cast:* Charles Dorety.
The Clean Up—August 17, 1921. Directed by William H. Watson. *Cast:* Charles Dorety.
Golfing—August 24, 1921. Written and directed by Fred C. Fishback. *Cast:* Brownie the dog. *Review:* MPW, September 3, 1921.
Brownie's Little Venus—September 11, 1921, Rivoli Theatre, NYC; September 14, 1921, nationwide. Directed by Fred Hibbard. *Cast:* Brownie the dog. *Reviews:* MPW, July 30, 1921; MPN, September 24, 1921.

Sea Shore Shapes—September 18, 1921, Central Theatre, NYC; October 19, 1921, nationwide. Directed by Alf Goulding. *Cast:* Teddy the dog, Louise Lorraine. *Review:* ETR, October 29, 1921.
A Week Off—September 28, 1921. Directed by Fred Hibbard. *Cast:* Charles Dorety. *Reviews:* ETR, October 8, 1921; MPW, October 15, 1921.
A Muddy Bride—October 2, 1921, Central Theatre, NYC; November 16, 1921, nationwide. Directed by Fred Hibbard. *Cast:* Jackie Morgan. *Review:* ETR, December 24, 1921.
Brownie's Baby Doll—October 5, 1921. Directed by Alf Goulding. *Cast:* Brownie the dog.
Teddy's Goat—November 30, 1921. Written and directed by Fred Hibbard. *Cast:* Teddy the dog, Charles Dorety, Bud Jamison, Viola Dolan. *Reviews:* ETR/MPW, December 17, 1921; MPN, December 24, 1921.
Get-Rich-Quick Peggy—October 23, 1921, Central Theatre, NYC; December 7, 1921, nationwide. Directed by Alf Goulding. *Cast:* Louise Lorraine, Aulbert Twins, Teddy the dog.
Chums—December, 18, 1921, Rivoli Theatre, NYC; December 28, 1921,

nationwide. Directed by Fred Hibbard. *Cast:* Brownie the dog. *Reviews:* ETR/MPW, January 7, 1922.

The Straphanger—January 11, 1922. Directed by Fred Hibbard. *Cast:* Lee Moran, Bartine Burkett. *Review:* ETR, January 21, 1922.

Circus Clowns—January 25, 1922. Directed by Fred Hibbard. *Cast:* Brownie the dog, William Irving. *Review:* MPN, February 11, 1922. *Preserved by:* Museum of Modern Art, New York.

Little Miss Mischief—February 15, 1922. Directed by Arvid Gillstrom. *Reviews:* ETR, February 25, 1922; MPN, March 18, 1922.

Peggy, Behave!—February 27, 1922, Central Theatre, NYC; March 15, 1922, nationwide. Written and directed by Arvid Gillstrom. *Review:* ETR, March 25, 1922.

The Little Rascal—April 23, 1922, Rivoli Theatre, NYC; May 24, 1922, nationwide. Written and directed by Arvid Gillstrom. *Cast:* Blanche Payson. *Production title:* The Little Angel.

Tips—June 11, 1922, Rivoli Theatre, NYC; July 25, 1932, nationwide. Directed by Arvid Gillstrom. *Cast:* Fred Spencer, Jack Henderson, Inez McDonnell, Pal the dog. *Locations:* the Ambassador Hotel in Los Angeles.

Peg o' the Movies—January 28, 1923, Rivoli Theatre, NYC; March 28, 1923, nationwide. Directed by Alf Goulding. *Cast:* Alf Goulding, Jr., Max Asher, Joe Bonner. *Reviews:* ETR, February 10 and March 24, 1923; MPW, February 10, 1923. *Production title:* The Baby Star.

Sweetie—February 11, 1923, Criterion Theatre, NYC; April 25, 1923, nationwide. Directed by Alf Goulding. *Cast:* Louise Lorraine, Max Asher, Jennie the organ grinder monkey. *Reviews:* ETR/MPN/MPW, February 24, 1923. *Production title:* Peggy Immigrates. *Preserved by:* Museum of Modern Art, New York.

The Kid Reporter—May 30, 1923. Directed by Alf Goulding. *Cast:* Blanche Payson, Albert Willis, Jim Kelly, Buddy Williams. *Reviews:* ETR/MPN/MPW, June 9, 1923. *Production title:* Peggy's Scoop, The Cub Reporter. *Preserved by:* National Film Archive, London.

Taking Orders—June 27, 1923. Directed by Alf Goulding. *Cast:* Dick Smith, Fred Spencer, Juanita Vaughn, Max Asher. *Reviews:* MPN, June 23, 1923; MPW, July 7, 1923. *Production title:* Peggy's Busy Day, Peggy's Restaurant.

Carmen, Jr.—June 28, 1923, on the Loew's circuit; August 29, 1923, nationwide. Directed by Alf Goulding. Titles by Joe W. Farnham. *Cast:* Lillian Hackett, Inez McDonnell, Thomas Wonder. *Location:* the mission at San Fernando Rey. *Production titles:* The Sênorita; Sunny Smiles.

Nobody's Darling—July 15, 1923, Rivoli's Theatre; September 29, 1923, nationwide. Directed by Alf Goulding and Harry Edwards. Written by William Friedle. *Cast:* Lillian Worth, Charlotte Rich, John Ralston. *Reviews:* ETR/MPN/MPW, August 4, 1923. *Production title:* The Orphan.

Little Miss Hollywood—October 31, 1923. Written and directed by Albert Herman. Titles by Joe W.

Farnham. *Cast:* Fred Spencer, Dick Smith, Joe Bonner, Florence Lee, Mary Pickford, Douglas Fairbanks, Charles Ray. *Note:* after the production of Baby Peggy's "last" short comedy, Century put together this "tour" of various Hollywood studios using stock footage.

Miles of Smiles—November 28, 1923. Directed by Alf Goulding. *Reviews:* ETR, October 27 and December 1, 1923; MPN, December 1, 1923. *Preserved by:* Museum of Modern Art, New York and Nederlands Filmmuseum, Amsterdam.

Hansel and Gretel—December 26, 1923. Written and directed by Alf Goulding. *Cast:* Jack Earle, Buddy Williams, Blanche Payson, Jim Kelly. *Review:* ETR, December 29, 1923.

Such Is Life—January 30, 1924. Directed by Alf Goulding. *Cast:* Joe Bonner, Thomas Wonder, Jack Henderson, Arnold MacDonald, Paul Stanhope. *Reviews:* ETR/MPW, February 2, 1924. *Production titles:* The Little Match Girl; Little Miss Spunk.

Peg o' the Mounted—February 27, 1924. Directed by Alf Goulding. Story "Sweetheart of the Mounted" by Bert Sterling. *Cast:* Bert Sterling, Jack Earle, Tiny Tim the pony. *Reviews:* ETR, November 3, 1923; MPN/MPW, March 1, 1924. *Locations:* Camp Curry in Yosemite National Park and the mission at San Fernando Rey. *Production title:* Peggy of the Mounted.

Our Pet—May 11, 1924. Directed by Herman Raymaker. *Cast:* Newton Hall, Winston Radom, Verne Winter, Donald Condon. *Production titles:* Too Many Lovers; Five After One.

The Flower Girl—May 25, 1924. Directed by Herman Raymaker. *Cast:* Billy Franey, Juanita Vaughn, Jack Earle, Joe Moore.

Stepping Some—June 8, 1924. Directed by Arvid Gillstrom. *Cast:* Ena Gregory, Inez McDonnell, Max Mogi, Tom Dempsey, Harry Asher, Blanche Payson. *Location:* The Bernheimer Estate in Hollywood. *Production titles:* Western Union; The Messenger Boy.

Poor Kid—June 22, 1924. Directed by Arvid Gillstrom. *Cast:* Max Asher.

Jack and the Beanstalk—July 7, 1924. Written and directed by Alf Goulding. *Cast:* Jack Earle, Blanche Payson, Buddy Williams.

Little Red Riding Hood—November 21, 1925. Written and directed by Alf Goulding. *Cast:* Peter the Great (the dog), Louise Lorraine, Arthur Trimble, Johnny Fox, Alf Goulding, Jr. *Review:* ETR, December 5, 1925. *Note:* This film was heavily promoted as the first in a prestigious series of Baby Peggy "fairy tails" for distribution in the Fall of 1922; however production problems, including a fire at the studio which damaged the original negative, delayed its release until after Baby Peggy had left the studio.

Unrealized Century Comedies

Grandma's Girl—in production 1922. Written and directed by Alf Goulding. *Cast:* Florence Lee, Jimmy Kelly. *Note:* this production, a satire of Harold Lloyd's hit *Grandma's Boy*, was first shut down due to illness which struck Baby Peggy and Alf Goulding, and was then canceled after a fire at the studio.

Newsreel Appearances

Screen Snapshots, second series, #14. December 1921. Produced by Screen Snapshots Inc. Distributed states rights by Federated Exchanges of America, Inc. Baby Peggy appears at home. Other celebrities featured include Wallace Reid, Harry Carey, Mary MacLaren, Richard Barthelmess, Mary Pickford and Douglas Fairbanks [Sr.], Constance Talmadge, Bessie Love, Pal the dog. Review under the title "There's No Place Like Home": MPN, December 17, 1921. *Preserved by:* Library of Congress, Washington, D.C.

Screen Snapshots, third series, #3. July 1922. Produced by Screen Snapshots Inc. Distributed states rights by Pathe Exchanges, Inc. Other celebrities featured include Buster Keaton, Snub Pollard, Marie Mosquini, Nell Shipman, Colleen Moore, Bryant Washburn, Pauline Stark, Ruth Clifford, Bessie Love, Carmel Myers. *Review:* MPW, July 1, 1922.

Screen Snapshots, third series, #21. March 1923. Produced by Screen Snapshots Inc. Distributed states rights by Pathe Exchanges, Inc. Baby Peggy is mobbed by "fans" Harold Lloyd, William Desmond and Gaston Blass. Other celebrities featured include Edna Flugrath, Shirley Mason, Viola Dana, Marion Davies, Louise Lovely, Milton Sills, Betty Compson, Jesse Lasky, Adolf Zukor and Marcus Loew. *Reviews:* ETR/MPW, March 10, 1923.

International News, #23. March 13, 1923. Produced by International News Reel Corp. Distributed by Universal. Baby Peggy appears with Irene Castle and at home with her sister, Louise. Press releases: ETR, March 24, 1923; MPN, March 31, 1923.

Screen Snapshots, fourth series, #3. November 1923. Produced by Screen Snapshots Inc. Distributed states rights by C.B.C. Film Sales, Inc. Other celebrities featured include Douglas Fairbanks, Jr., Charles Ray, Wallace Beery, Teddy the dog. *Review:* MPN, November 17, 1923.

Screen Snapshots, fourth series, #8. January 1924. Produced by Screen Snapshots Inc. Distributed states rights by C.B.C. Film Sales, Inc. Baby Peggy visits New York City. Other celebrities featured include Rudolph Valentino, Bobby Vernon, Dorothy Dalton, Agnes Ayres, Earle Kenton, Creighton Hale, Wandy Hawley, Richard Dix, Lottie Pickford, Dagmar Godowsky, Irving Cummings, Herbert Rawlinson, Hope Hampton, Bessie Love. Press release: MPN, January 5, 1924.

Screen Snapshots, fourth series, #16. April 1924. Produced by Screen Snapshots Inc. Distributed states rights by C.B.C. Film Sales, Inc. Other celebrities featured include Jackie Coogan, Mae Murray, Marguerite De La Motte, David Warfield, Douglas Fairbanks [Sr.]. Press release: MPN, April 26, 1924.

[Life in Hollywood] (ca 1923–1924) Goodwill Pictures Inc. produced by L. M. BeDell. With Lon Chaney, Ed Brady, Pat O'Malley,

Bob Hill, Max Davidson, Neely Edwards, Bert Roach, Hobart Henley, King Baggott, Irving Cummings, Harry Pollard, Pete Morrison, Emmett Corrigan, Edward Sedgwick, Hoot Gibson, Mary Philbin, Margaret Morris, Reginald Denny, Joe Martin. *Note:* Baby Peggy is featured together with director Jesse Robbins on the set of *The Law Forbids*. Original production credits for this tour of Universal studios are lacking on the reissued sound version in circulation on video.

Silent Features

Penrod—1922. Marshall Neilan Productions/Associated First National Pictures. Directed by Marshall Neilan. Screenplay by Lucita Squier, based on Booth Tarkington's "Penrod" and "Penrod, a Comedy in Four Acts." Photographed by David Kesson and Ray June. *Cast:* Wesley Barry, Tully Marshall, Claire McDowell, John Harron, Sunshine Morrison.

Fool's First—1922. Marshall Neilan Productions/Associated First National Pictures. Directed by Marshall Neilan. Screenplay by Marion Fairfax, based on the short story "Fool's First" by Hugh MacNair Kahler. Titles by Hugh Wiley. Photographed by David Kesson and Karl Struss. *Cast:* Richard Dix, Claire Windsor, Claude Gillingwater, Raymond Griffith.

Hollywood—1923. Famous Players Lasky/Paramount Pictures. Directed by James Cruze. Story by Frank Condon. Adaptation by Tom Geraghty. Photographed by Karl Brown. *Cast:* Hope Drown, Luke

Cosgrave, George K. Arthur, and over seventy guest stars and celebrities including Baby Peggy as herself.

The Darling of New York—1923. Universal Pictures. Directed by King Baggot. Story by King Baggot. Screenplay by Raymond L. Schrock. Photographed by John Stumar. *Cast:* Sheldon Lewis, Gladys Brockwell, Pat Hartigan, Frank Currier, Junior Coughlan. *Production titles:* Wanted, a Home; Whose Baby Are You?

The Law Forbids—1924. Universal Pictures. Directed by Jesse Robbins. Story by Bernard McConville. Screenplay by Lois Zellner and Ford I. Beebe. Photographed by Charles Kaufman and Jack Stevens. *Cast:* Robert Ellis, Elinor Fair, Winifred Bryson, James Corrigan. *Production titles:* Settled Out of Court; The Right to Love.

Captain January—1924. Principal Pictures. Directed by Edward F. Cline. Screenplay by Eve Unsell and John Grey. Photographed by Glen MacWilliams. *Cast:* Hobart Bosworth, Irene Rich, Lincoln Stedman, Harry T. Morey. *Locations:* Laguna Beach, California. Preserved at: Archives du Film du CNC, Bois d'Arcy, France/Library of Congress, Washington, D.C.

The Family Secret—1924. Universal Pictures. Directed by William A. Seiter. Based on Frances Hodgson Burnett's "Editha's Burglar." Screenplay by Lois Zellner. Photographed by John Stumar. *Cast:* Gladys Hulette, Edward Earle, Frank Currier, Cesare Gravina. *Production title:* The Burglar's Kid.

Helen's Babies—1924. Principal Pictures. Directed by William A.

Seiter. Adaptation by Hope Lor-
ing and Louis D. Leighton. Photo-
graphed by William Daniels and
Glen MacWilliams. *Cast:* Clara
Bow, Jean Carpenter, Edward
Everett Horton, Claire Adams.
Preserved by: Library of Congress,
Washington, D.C. and National
Film Archive, London.
April Fool—1926. Chadwick Pic-
tures. Directed by Nat Ross.
Screenplay by Zion Myer. Pho-
tographed by L. William O'Con-
nell. *Cast:* Alexander Carr, Duane
Thompson, Mary Alden, Ray-
mond Keane.

Sound Films

Off His Base—1932. Educational
Pictures Inc. Produced by Norman
L. Sper and James Gleason. Story
by Charles W. Paddock. Directed
by James Gleason. *Cast:* James
Gleason, Lucille Gleason, Russell
Gleason, Eugene Palette. 2 reels.
Hollywood on Parade #3—1932.
Paramount Pictures. *Cast:* Benny
Rubin, Neil Hamilton, Gary
Cooper, Fifi Dorsay, Tom Mix. 1 reel
Hollywood on Parade—1932. Para-
mount Pictures. *Cast:* Frankie Darro
and the "Our Gang" kids. 1 reel.
Eight Girls in a Boat—1934. Charles
R. Rogers Productions, Inc./Para-
mount Productions, Inc. Directed
by Richard Wallace. Story by Hel-
mut Brandis. Adaptation by Lewis
Foster. Screenplay by Casey Rob-
inson. Photographed by Gilbert

Warrenton. *Cast:* Dorothy Wilson,
Douglass Montgomery, Kay John-
son and Peggy (as a Swiss board-
ing school girl).
Ah! Wilderness—1935. Metro-Gold-
wyn-Meyer. Directed by Clarence
Brown. Based on the play by Eugene
O'Neill. Screenplay by Frances
Goodrich and Albert Hackett. Pho-
tographed by Clyde de Vinna. *Cast:*
Wallace Beery, Lionel Barrymore,
Aline MacMahon, Mickey Rooney,
and Peggy (as a schoolgirl in the
graduation sequence).
Girls' Dormitory—1936. 20th Cen-
tury-Fox. Directed by Irving Cum-
mings. Screenplay by Gene Markey.
Photographed by Merritt Gerstad.
Cast: Herbert Marshall, Ruth
Chatterton, Simone Simon, Tyrone
Power, and Peggy (as a schoolgirl).

Television Appearances

Whatever Became of Hollywood? 1974,
Canada. CBC. Documentary on
child stars.
Babes in Hollywood. 1975, Great Bri-
tain. BBC. Directed by Cris Cook.
To Tell the Truth. 1976, USA. Game
Show, syndicated.
The Joyce Davidson Show. 1979, Canada.
National TV. Two-part interview,
March 16–17.
Hollywood's Children. 1982, USA. Wom-
bat Productions/PBS broadcast.
60 Minutes. 1985, Australia. Inter-
view.
When We Were Young. 1989, USA.
PBS fundraiser on child stars.

Note: With one exception, this filmography does not include Baby Peggy's uncredited appearances.

Priscilla Bonner

I first spoke to Priscilla Bonner from her nursing home facility in California. She was 96 years old and I had written her a note. She responded by mail and gave me her phone number, and thus ensued many telephone conversations with this remarkable woman. While she told me fascinating stories about other big stars, I soon realized her story, too, needed to be documented. And while she has been written about before, I feel privileged to have been the last to interview Miss Bonner and reprint here her most fascinating insights into a young Hollywood.

BEFORE HOLLYWOOD

Priscilla Bonner was born in Washington, D.C., on February 17, 1899. "My mother's family all lived in Washington. I was raised by the same nurse who raised my mother and she never worked for any other family in her life.

"I remember one day I was sitting on her lap, I was very small. There was an electrical storm [with] very great thunder and lightning. I said, 'Oh Vinnie! What is that terrible noise?!' And she said, 'It's the voice of the Lord!' It scared me and I'm still scared and very afraid of thunder."

When Priscilla was sixteen events happened which would eventually lead her to Hollywood. "My mother was a very devout Episcopalian. I was going away to a little girls' school in Washington, Episcopalian, and one of the other girls was going to dancing school. I wrote my father and asked him if I could go and take lessons at the school. My father was so easy that it wasn't any problem; he wrote back and gave me a check which I think was ten dollars, to take lessons.

Priscilla Bonner in 1925.

"One day a man came over and said he was looking for a girl. So all the girls came out and danced for him and he picked me! I was just what he wanted. I was tall and blonde and also, I could *dance!* He wasn't a very big man and he danced with me, you know, he tried me out. 'I can teach you everything I want to teach you in a week,' he said.

"And I'll tell you something, if you want to know what heaven is, I can tell you all about it because I've been there! He had a contract with the Orpheum Circuit. I was in heaven right there! To go out and work in the Orpheum Circuit and dance for people was my idea of heaven. [The Circuit toured vaudeville acts between films.]

"Then he said, 'How old are you?' 'I'm sixteen.' His face fell. He couldn't take anybody out under eighteen and I couldn't sign a contract. So the next day at school I wrote a letter to my mother and asked her if she would please come home and go with me on the wonderful, *wonderful* thing that had happened to me. The telegram came. I didn't open it because in those days the only time a telegram came was when somebody died! It just lay there.

"Now there were two girls in my room and one whose name was Abigail came in and said, 'Priscilla, there's a telegram here on the dresser.' I said, 'Yeah, yeah I know it, I know it.' 'Well there's somebody dead!' she said. 'I don't want to know who it is. I've seen my mother so young and beautiful and my father is so young and handsome, I just can't believe it. I don't want to know who it is!'

"'*I'm* going to open the telegram,' Abigail said. So she opened it and the telegram said: 'MOTHER ARRIVING THURSDAY!' So mother arrived and the whole family got together. As far as they were concerned, the Orpheum Circuit was a den of iniquity and that I should go off wasn't even worth discussing. So I had to turn it down but I was determined! I never let up for a minute and when I was eighteen, my father said, 'Let her do what she wants to do. If you have not succeeded and are not supporting yourself in a year, will you promise you will come home?'

"I said, 'Yes father, if you let me go.' So we both stood up, very solemnly, and we shook hands. You have my solemn oath of honor."

During this time Priscilla and her family were in Chicago. Her father was in the Army on General Leonard Wood's staff. There was another general who had a daughter with friends in Los Angeles. Priscilla, invited to be a paying guest of the family in Los Angeles, headed for California. Soon she would be on the MGM lot.

BLONDE, YOUNG AND INNOCENT

"I went over to MGM and I was very nicely dressed, mother saw to that. My hair was down my back and I was blonde. I *never* wore my hair in a bob. I had no make-up on and the man at the office said, 'Well what do *you* want?' I said, 'I just came out from the east and I want to go into pictures and I would like you to take me.'

"And he was so surprised that he took me in to the casting director! It was *unbelievable!* I was so young and so innocent looking and so sweet. And that was just what I was: just a nice, innocent young girl and that's what I looked like. So the man said, 'Are you out here without your mother?' And I said yes.

"He said, 'Jesus Christ!' and I said, 'Oh, I am not used, to such language!' My father *never* spoke that way in front of my mother. So he said he was sorry and then called his secretary and in said, 'This here, um, um, young lady...' I think he realized he had to speak more carefully in front of me. 'Take this young lady over to see Mr. Green, they're looking for someone with a face like she has.' [Mr. Alfred E. Green was apparently an assistant to casting director Jack Robertson, actor Cliff Robertson's father.]

"So the secretary walked me across the lot. It was a long distance, and into an office. She said to 'sit here in this chair and someone will come in a few minutes.'"

JACK PICKFORD

"So I sat there and all of a sudden a young man came in the door. He stood there and looked at me and I looked at him and he looked at me and

A striking Priscilla Bonner, circa 1924 (Melbourne Spurr Hollywood, courtesy of Bill Barbour).

neither one of us said a word. All of a sudden I realized it was Jack Pickford! I was so awestruck that I couldn't talk. My tongue closed to the roof of my mouth and I just *looked* at him. I couldn't believe what was happening to me! Then he turned around and walked out.

"The girl came back and took me to the office and the casting director said, 'Mr. Pickford likes you and we're going to give you the part of his leading lady. And he knows that you don't have any experience but you've got the face that he wanted. He'll work with you.' And that's the way it started.

[Miss Bonner's first featured film was *Homer Comes Home* (1920) with Charles Ray. She would, however, eventually work with Jack Pickford and her affection for him was very apparent.]

"I played the lead with Jack Pickford in *The Man Who Had Everything* [1920]. Jack was a very fine actor and he was a very, very warm personality, a very charming person."

WILL ROGERS

"I worked with Will Rogers and Mary Alden. I played Will Rogers' daughter and the name of the picture was *Honest Hutch* [1920]. Will Rogers was certainly not glamorous and he certainly was *not* sexy, but he was *unique*. There is no one like him and there will *never* be again. He was very polite and he never used the words that are in common use now, never! And Mary Alden, who was in *Birth of a Nation* [1915], played my mother."

VALENTINO

"As far as Valentino was concerned, I do not believe he had an affair with Pola Negri. I'll tell you, he was not a chaser, he did not have that reputation."

Virginia Brown Faire was Priscilla's "dearest and closest friend." It was on the set of *Peter Pan* [1924], in which Virginia played Tinkerbell, that Priscilla had the opportunity to get to know Hollywood's "Latin Lover." Virginia's mother, Mrs. Brown, was also of Italian heritage, Brown being her married name. Valentino spent a lot of time with her on the set "talking Italian, and Mrs. Brown was very fond of him."

"Virginia was only fourteen and her mother was always with her. During the filming of *Peter Pan* [Mary Brian played Wendy and Betty

William Collier, Jr., and Virginia Brown Faire, Bonner's "dearest friend."

Bronson, Peter Pan], three of the wires broke leaving poor Virginia dangling in the air.

"Mrs. Brown was hysterical. 'They're *killing* my baby!' Virginia was hanging by one leg up in the air and she kept saying, 'Mother please, don't act so. I'm all right, oh please be quiet, you're embarrassing me!'

"Somebody got a ladder and as I remember it, I think Valentino ran up the ladder and grabbed hold of Virginia and held her up until they could cut the other wires and let her down. Then she came over to her mother, who by this time was screaming, and she said to her, 'You're just embarrassing me and *please*, don't be so *Italian!*'

"Then Valentino said, 'Oh Virginia, don't speak that way to your mother,' and he got a chair for Mrs. Brown, trying to console her. Does that sound to you like a 'chaser'? No, I can tell you he was not. I just happened to know about Valentino and I'll tell you he did *not* have a reputation of being a chaser. Besides that, I think he was a little bit in awe of

Silent screen superstar Pola Negri in 1924.

Pola Negri. Negri was very beautiful, but then Virginia was, too, except she was four-teen.

"Valentino was not in the picture but was watching and he sat with Mrs. Brown all the time. He didn't go and sit with all of the young peo-ple; he would rather sit with her. Mrs. Brown told me, she said, 'Rudolpho's homesick,' she called him Rudolpho, not Rudolph. She said, 'He misses his mother and that's why he wants to sit with me.' And she said, 'He's very polite and his mother raised him nicely.'

"Whenever Mrs. Brown would be on the set, he would always find a chair for her to sit in, nobody else cared but *he* did. Virginia and I were always together and Mrs. Brown said

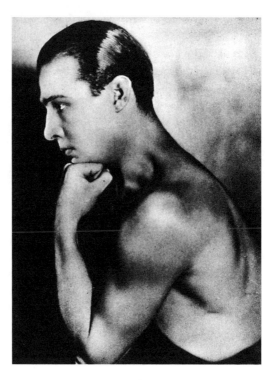

Rudolph Valentino in 1924.

to me, 'He's a lonesome, homesick boy and he comes and wants to talk to me in Italian. Of course I enjoy it because my English isn't too good. So we just sit and visit and he's not a girl chaser but he *is* a wonderful dancer.'

"'And when he dances with a woman, it's like making love to her, because he dances with his whole body.' And that's true. He was the most *superb* dancer I *ever* saw in my life. He was just so graceful and wonderful. When he would take a woman in his arms and dance with her, especially in something like say, a waltz, it was a beautiful thing to watch. But he didn't chase girls!

"He was married twice. His first wife left him, I do not know why. Maybe because he was so poor, maybe because she just got tired of being poor. But then later on, he made a hit [a likely reference to *The Four Horse-men of the Apocalypse*, 1921]. And Mrs. Brown said, 'He looks like many other fine Italian young men. He's nice looking and he's been very nicely brought up. He had a very good mother who taught him good manners and he knows how to behave. He's very courteous to women but he's *not a chaser!*'

"Virginia was my dearest friend and I knew her mother from the time Virginia was fourteen years old. She died when Virginia was about thirty. Mrs. Brown was a typical Italian, very excitable. Virginia was embarrassed with her mother's screaming and yelling and total pandemonium. I thought it was all very amusing!"

CLARA BOW

"I never worked at Paramount until I was loaned out to work in a picture with Clara Bow. I did not want to support a feminine star. I thought I had gone *beyond* that, but they forced me to. That's the only time I worked for Paramount and the picture was called *It* [1927].

"She was very professional and very nice, very pleasant to work with. And she was very afraid of her father. He was a character and threw his weight around. He talked too loud and she said, 'Yes papa, yes papa." I think he was trying to run everything. I'm not sure. I think that's why she got married so young. I think she wanted to get away from him."

EARLY WORKING CONDITIONS

"I can remember one time with Will Rogers, we went up to the Sacramento River to make some locations. It was *so* hot up there. I can still remember how we suffered and you know, he never complained. We were working on a boat on the river. They were photographing the river and scenery on both sides to show it was supposed to be in the south. We were up there for about a week I think. A week of *horror*. It was hot, hot, hot! It was awful.

"Of course it was warm inside too. The [klieg] lights were very warm. I had hemorrhaging of the retina from the lights. There were several reasons that I stopped working when I did and that was one of them. And don't forget, we didn't have air conditioning then. We used fans of course, but the stages were very hot.

"We worked all day on a film and sometimes on into the night. If we were working on a stage it didn't matter. Sometimes we had to 'kill a set' so that another picture could come in the next day so we had to work on through the evening. Of course there weren't any unions like they have now so we *worked*, believe me we did. We earned our money. But if you look at some of the early pictures, the camera work was *beautiful!*"

FILM FOLK

"I met D.W. Griffith at Preston Sturges' home but I cannot say that I knew him. I said, 'How do you do sir.' That's not knowing a person. I was very fond of [director] Frank Capra. He was so easy and quiet. And Reginald Barker. Jerry Storm was a very nice, easy director. It was a pleasure to work with him. Most directors have very strong, warm personalities so they can handle people well.

"I worked in two pictures with Tom Moore. He was a star at MGM and a little vain. He was very attractive and a very good actor. Also Owen Moore who was a dramatic actor. [Owen was Mary Pickford's first husband. Actor Henry Walthall in a 1931 interview in *New Movie* magazine tells a cute story: "He fell in love with Mary, I think, as soon as she arrived (in New York). But she was a mere child and her mother kept close guard on her. Mary was so young and her mother was afraid that Owen would sweep her off her feet before she really knew her own mind. The two just stood and looked at each other. Somebody was always watching them and teasing them. They would get behind a piece of scenery once in awhile to have a few words alone, but it wasn't long ever before they were discovered."]

"They were all very gifted people. I was awestruck with everybody. I was interviewed for *Charley's Aunt* [1925] and Dorothy DeVore who was a star at Christie [studio] was very fond of me. She said she'd like to have me be in the picture and I don't know how much help that did but it certainly didn't hurt!

"There weren't so many parties because everybody got up very early. Five, six o'clock in the morning was the regular time to get up and many times earlier than that. You see when you work all day under hot lights, you're ready to come home and have a good dinner and go to sleep."

JOHN BARRYMORE: A SEA BEAST?

Priscilla Bonner had one of her greatest film successes in 1925. *Drusilla with a Million* only helped to support Hollywood's opinion that Bonner was an accomplished actress taking on more fulfilling roles. The film also features Mary Carr and Ken Harlan and with its success, she found an opportunity to work with another film giant, John Barrymore.

An early movie magazine clipping showed a lovely Priscilla Bonner with the following caption: "In *Drusilla with a Million*, this demure little player went over the top with such a dash that she's become 'Priscilla with a Million—Fans.' She's just been chosen by John Barrymore as leading lady for his new picture, *The Sea Beast*. It's the story of the New England whaling ships of 1840."

This proved an unfortunate experience for Priscilla and one which she could never forget. Had this film partnership worked, it clearly would have elevated her career to a higher level of stardom.

"I had worked in a picture with Harry Langdon called *The Strong Man* [1926] and it was directed by Frank Capra. I played the romantic lead. It was a very small part but it was important and I was singled out for considerable praise.

"I was offered the lead with John Barrymore in *The Sea Beast* [1925] and then I was thrown out. I thought I could get there with just my ability but I realized I couldn't. I had great confidence in myself and I knew I was talented but I *wasn't* willing to give personal favors and that was the thing he demanded.

"It's the truth. It's a very bad subject for me. Dolores Costello [whom Barrymore later married] was given the part. She wore all my clothes that were fitted for me! It was terrible. I think it did something awful to me. I knew the talent wasn't enough.

"He not only wasn't gentlemanly, he was dirty! He picked his nose all the time. He was 'Mr. Hyde' if you know what I mean. He was quite a drinker. His face was red with blotches. I was *shocked* and deathly afraid of him. He fired me. He didn't want me once he saw he couldn't have me. I made up my mind to quit pictures and marry. The experienced disheartened me you know, with John Barrymore."

Bonner was only one of the many "conquests" for Barrymore, who liked his women *and* the bottle. German actress Camilla Horn remembers her experience with him in a 1974 interview with John Kobal. The film was *The Tempest* (1928). "Sometimes he was drunk. And when we were dancing together in one scene, he fell down with me on the floor because he was so drunk. So they had to build a carousel affair for us, he sat on one side, me on the other, it was a sort of criss-cross arrangement, and we put our arms around each other, looked deeply into our eyes and somebody moved the carousel around so it looked in the film as if we were lost in each other's arms. He was married to Dolores Costello at the time—a beautiful soft featured blonde, exquisite, so he didn't try to make any passes at me."

MARRIAGE AND LEAVING FILMS

"I finally earned a very good living and my family all came out here to Los Angeles. Various things happened, some of them nice things, some of them heartbreaking. It's a heartbreaking business. I never worked in my life until I worked in pictures. I was in school. I made around forty or fifty pictures. I was very busy working all the time.

"I got married in 1928 to Dr. E. Bertrand Woolfan. I must say, I was happily married and never regretted marrying. He was a remarkable man, brilliant and successful. I had a very happy life with him and that's what I wanted. I was in love, I think I did the right thing. I led the normal life of a young bride in love with her husband, entertaining for him, doing for him, that's what I wanted.

"There's nothing good about being old. When you're young, that's the time you should enjoy your life and I did. I *thoroughly* enjoyed my work in pictures and meeting everyone I met. They were all gifted or they wouldn't have reached the position they did."

Miss Bonner never made talking films but assured me she could have. "I wouldn't have been afraid, I think that my voice would have been all right, it would have carried. That hadn't anything to do with [retiring]."

It's important to note that Priscilla Bonner's sister Marjorie also was an actress in silent films, though she never attained the celebrity of Priscilla. "I lacked Priscilla's ambition," she once reported to an interviewer.

A 1925 movie mag was quick to point out their differences: "Marjorie is a saucy, bob-haired flapper with sophisticated pretensions, who

Cinema sisters Marjorie (left) and Priscilla Bonner in later years (Long Photography).

has trained her rosebud lips into the cynical curl now the mode for young things. She longs to play deep, stark tragedy-soulful characters such as her idol, Lillian Gish. Priscilla, on the other hand, seems to belong in an aristrocratic drawing room. She might be a younger edition of Claire Windsor. She is synonymous with chiffons and light shimmering things. And she longs to play bitter, hard creatures. It was in such a role in *Tarnish* [1924] that she gave her most skillful performance."

Miss Bonner was a delight to talk with. Her notes and her memories presented a wonderful opportunity to further document this most important early actress. I was saddened to learn of her passing on February 26, 1996. But I was reminded of the 1950 classic *Sunset Boulevard* when Joe Gillis (William Holden) looks out at the empty swimming pool and remembers all the stars who swam there "ten thousand midnights ago." Bonner would have been among them. She was 97.

FILMOGRAPHY

Honest Hutch—1920. Goldwyn Pictures Corp. *Distributor:* Goldwyn Distributing Corp. 5 reels. *Director:* Clarence G. Badger. *Scenario:* Arthur F. Statter. *Camera:* Marcel Le Picard. *Cast:* Will Rogers, Mary Alden, Priscilla Bonner, Tully Marshall, Nick Cogley, Byron Munson, Eddie Trebaol, Jeanette Trebaol, Yves Trebaol. *Note:* The working title of this film was *Old Hutch.*

The Man Who Had Everything—1920. Goldwyn Pictures Corp. *Distributor:* Goldwyn Distributing Corp., Oct. 1920 [Goldwyn Pictures Corp., 5 reels]. *Director:* Alfred E. Green. *Assistant Director:* Billy Reiter. *Scenario:* Arthur F. Statter, Cam Blyde Cook. *Cast:* Jack Pickford, Lionel Belmore,

Priscilla Bonner, Shannon Day, Alec B. Francis, William Machin.

The Son of Wallingford—1921. Vitagraph Co. of America. 35mm. 8 reels, 7,851 feet. *Director/Story/Scenario:* George Randolph Chester, Mrs. George Randolph Chester. *Photographer:* Stephen Smith, Jr. *Cast:* Wilfrid North, Tom Gallery, George Webb, Antrim Short, Van Dyke Brooke, Sidney D'Albrook, Andrew Arbuckle, Bobby Mack, Walter Rodgers, Priscilla Bonner, Florence Hart, Lila Leslie, Margaret Cullington, Martha Mattox.

Bob Hampton of Placer—May, 1921. Marshall Neilan Productions. *Distributor:* Associated First National Pictures. Silent. B&W. 35mm. *Producer/Director:* Marshall Neilan. *Scenario:* Marion Fairfax.

Photographer: Jacques Bizeul, David Kesson. *Art Director:* Ben Carre. *Cast:* James Kirkwood, Wesley Barry, Marjorie Daw, Pat O'Malley, Noah Beery, Frank Leigh, Dwight Crittenden, Tom Gallery, Priscilla Bonner, Charles West, Bert Sprotte, Carrie Clark Ward, Vic Potel, Buddy Post.

Home Stuff—June, 1921. Silent. B&W. 35mm. 6 reels. *Director:* Albert Kelley. *Story/Scenario:* Frank Daxey, Agnes Christine Johnson. *Photographer:* John Arnold. *Art Director:* A.F. Mantz. *Cast:* Viola Dana, Tom Gallery, Josephine Crowell, Nelson McDowell, Priscilla Bonner, Robert Chandler, Aileen Manning, Philip Sleeman.

Shadows—November, 1922. Preferred Pictures. *Distributor:* Al Lichtman Corp. 10 November 1922. [c7 October 1922]. Silent. B&W. 35mm. 7 reels, 7,040 feet. *Presented by:* B.P. Schulberg. *Director:* Tom Forman. *Scenario:* Eve Unsell, Hope Loring. *Photography:* Harry Perry. *Cast:* Lon Chaney, Marguerite De La Motte, Harrison Ford, John Sainpolis, Walter Long, Buddy Messenger, Frances Raymond, Priscilla Bonner, Frances Raymond.

April Showers—1923. Preferred Pictures. Silent. B&W. 35mm. 6 reels, 6,350 feet. *Presented by:* B.P. Schulberg. *Producer:* B.P. Schulberg. *Director:* Tom Forman. *Story/Scenario:* Hope Loring, Louis D. Lighton. *Photography:* Harry Perry. *Cast:* Colleen Moore, Kenneth Harlan, Ruth Clifford, Priscilla Bonner, Myrtle Vane, James Corrigan, Jack Byron, Ralph Faulkner, Tom McGuire, Kid McCoy, Danny Goodman.

Purple Dawn—Charles R. Seeling. *Distributor:* Aywon Film Corp. May 1923 [New York showing]. Silent. B&W. 35mm. 5 reels, 4,850 feet. *Photography:* Raymond Walker, Vernon Walker. *Cast:* Bert Sprotte, William E. Aldrich, James B. Leong, Edward Piel, Bessie Love, William Horne, Priscilla Bonner.

Hold Your Breath—Christie Film Co. *Distributor:* W.W. Hodkinson Corp. 25 May, 1924 [c25 May 1924]. Silent. B&W. 6 reels, 5,900 feet. *Director:* Scott Sidney. *Story:* Frank Roland Conklin. *Photography:* Gus Peterson, Alex Phillips. *Technical Director:* Tom Brierley. *Cast:* Dorothy Devore, Walter Heirs, Tully Marshall, Jimmie Adams, Priscilla Bonner, Jimmy Harrison, Lincoln Plumer, Patricia Palmer, Rosa Gore, Jay Belasco, George Pierce, Victor Rodman, Budd Fine, Eddie Baker, Max Davidson.

Tarnish—1924. Goldwyn Pictures. *Distributor:* Associated First National Pictures. August 1924. Silent. B&W. 35mm. 7 reels, 6,831 feet. *Presented by:* Samuel Goldwyn. *Director:* George Fitzmaurice. *Scenario:* Frances Marion. *Photography:* William Tuers, Arthur Miller. *Technical Director:* Ben Carré. *Film Editor:* Stuart Heisler. *Cast:* May McAvoy, Ronald Colman, Marie Prevost, Albert Gran, Mrs. Russ Whytall, Priscilla Bonner, Harry Myer, Kay Deslys, Lydai Yeamans Titus, William Boyd, Snitz Edwards.

A Desperate Adventure—1924. Independent Pictures. Silent. B&W. 35mm. 5 reels, ca4,880 feet. *Presented by:* Jesse J.P. McGowan. *Story:* James Ormont. *Photography:*

Walter Griffin. *Cast:* Franklyn Farnu, Marie Walcamp, Priscilla Bonner.

Chalk Marks—1924. Peninsula Studios. *Distributing Producers:* Distributing Corp. Silent. B&W. 35mm. 7 reels, 6,711 feet. *Supervisor/Writer:* Frank E. Woods. *Director:* John G. Adolfi. *Photography:* Joseph Walker, Charles Kaufman. *Cast:* Marguerite Snow, Ramsey Wallace, June Elvidge, Lydia Knott, Rex Lease, Helen Ferguson, Priscilla Bonner, Harold Holland, Verna Mercereau, Fred Church, Lee Willard.

The White Desert—1925. Metro-Goldwyn Pictures. Silent. B&W. 35mm. 7 reels, 6,464 feet. *Presented by:* Louis B. Mayer. *Director:* Reginald Barker. *Scenario:* L.G. Rigby. *Adaptation:* Monte M. Katterjohn. *Comedy Relief:* Lew Lipton. *Photography:* Percy Hilburn. *Cast:* Claire Windsor, Pat O'Malley, Robert Frazer, Frank Currier, William Eugene, Roy Laidlaw, Sojin, Priscilla Bonner, Snitz Edwards, Milton Ross, Matthew Betz.

Drusilla with a Million—1925. Associated Arts Corp. *Distributor:* Film Booking Offices of America. Silent. BOW. 36mm. 7 reels, 7,391 feet. *Supervisor:* Ludwig G.B. Erb. *Director:* F. Harmon Weight. *Scenario:* Lois Zellner. *Photography:* Lyman Broening. *Assistant Director:* Thorton Freeland. *Cast:* Mary Carr, Priscilla Bonner, Kenneth Harlan, Henry Barrows, William Humphreys, Claire Du Brey.

The Mansion of Aching Hearts—1925. B.P. Schulberg Productions. Silent, B&W. 35mm. 6 reels, 6,147 feet. *Director:* James P. Hogan.

Adaptation: Frederick Stowers. *Photography:* Harry Perry. *Cast:* Ethel Clayton, Barbara Bedford, Priscilla Bonner, Philo McCullough, Edward Delaney, Cullen Landis, Sam De Grasse, Eddie Phillips, Edward Gribbon, Helen Hogo.

Red Kimono—1925. Mrs. Wallace Reid Productions. *Distributor:* Vital Exchanges. Silent. B&W. 35mm. 7 reels. *Director:* Walter Lang. *Adaptation:* Dorothy Arzner. *Story:* Adela Rogers St. Johns. *Photography:* James Diamond. *Cast:* Priscilla Bonner, Theodore von Eltz, Tyrone Power, Mary Carr, Virginia Pearson, Mrs. Wallace Reid.

Charley's Aunt—1925. Christie Film Co. *Distributing Producers:* Distributing Corp. Silent. B&W. 35mm. 8 reels, 7,243 feet. *Presented by:* Al Christie, Charles Christie. *Director:* Scott Sidney. *Scenario:* F. McGrew Willis. *Title:* Joseph Farnham. *Photography:* Gus Peterson, Paul Garnett. *Cast:* Sydney Chaplin, Ethel Shannon, James E. Page, Lucien Littlefield, Alex B. Francis, Phillips Smalley, Eulalie Jensen, David James, Jimmy Harrison, Mary Akin, Priscilla Bonner.

Eyes of Hollywood—1925. Chesterfield Motion Pictures. Silent. B&W. 35mm. 5 reels, 4,492 feet. *Cast:* Ward Wing, Priscilla Bonner.

Proud Flesh—1925. Metro-Goldwyn Pictures. Silent. B&W. 35mm. 7 reels, 5,770 feet. *Presented by:* Louis B. Mayer. *Director:* King Vidor. *Scenario:* Harry Behn, Agnes Christine Johnston. *Photography:* John Arnold. *Assistant Director:* David Howard. *Cast:* Eleanor Boardman, Pat O'Malley,

Harrison Ford, Trixie Friganza, William J. Kelly, Rosita Marstini, Evelyn Sherman, George Nichols, Margaret Seddon, Lillian Elliott, Priscilla Bonner.

Three Bad Men—1926. Fox Film Corp. Silent. B&W. 35mm. 9 reels, 8,710 feet. *Presented by:* William Fox. *Director:* John Ford. *Adaptation/ Scenario:* John Stone. *Title:* Ralph Spence, Malcolm Stuart Boylan. *Photographer:* George Schneiderman. *Assistant Director:* Edward O'Fearna. *Cast:* George O'Brien, Olive Borden, Lou Tellegen, J. Farrell MacDonald, Tom Santschi, Frank Campeau, George Harris, Jay Hunt, Priscilla Bonner, Otis Harlan, Walter Perry, Grace Gordon, Alex B. Francis, George Irving, Phyllis Haver, Vester Pegg, Bud Osborne.

The Strong Man—1926. Silent. B&W. 35mm. 7 reels, 6,882 feet. *Director:* Frank Capra. *Story:* Arthur Ripley. *Photographer:* Elgin Lessley, Glenn Kershner. *Comedy Construction:* Clarence Hennecke. *Cast:* Harry Langdon, Priscilla Bonner, Gertrude Astor, William V. Mong, Robert McKim, Arthur Thalasso.

The False Alarm—1926. Silent. B&W. 35mm. 6 reels, 5,235 feet. *Producer:* Harry Cohn. *Director:* Frank O'Connor. *Story/Scenario:* Leah Baird. *Photography:* Faxon M. Dean. *Cast:* Ralph Lewis, Dorothy Revier, John Harron, Mary Carr, George O'Hara, Priscilla Bonner, Lillian Leighton.

The Earth Woman—1926. Mrs. Wallace Reid Productions. *Distributor:* Associated Exhibitors. Silent. B&W. 35mm. 6 reels, 5,380 feet. *Producer:* Mrs. Wallace Reid.

Director: Walter Lang. *Story:* Norton S. Parker. *Photographer:* Milton Moore. *Cast:* Mary Alden, Priscilla Bonner, Russell Simpson, Carroll Nye, Joe Butterworth, John Carr, Johnny Walker, William Scott.

The Prince of Headwaiters—1927. Sam E. Rork Productions. *Distributor:* First National Pictures. Silent. B&W. 35mm. 7 reels, 6,400 feet. *Presented by:* Sam E. Rork. *Director:* John Francis Dillon. *Adaptation:* Jane Murfin. *Photographer:* James Van Trees. *Cast:* Lewis Stone, Priscilla Bonner, E.J. Ratcliffe, Lilyan Tashman, John Patrick, Robert Agnew, Ann Rork, Cleve Moore, Dick Folkens, Lincoln Stedman, Cecille Evans, Marion McDonald, Nita Cavalier.

Paying the Price—1927. Columbia Pictures. Silent. B&W. 35mm. 6 reels, 5,558 feet. *Producer:* Harry Cohn. *Director:* David Selman. *Scenario:* Dorothy Howell. *Photographer:* George Meehan. *Cast:* Marjorie Bonner, Priscilla Bonner, John Miljan, George Hackathorne, Mary Carr, Eddie Phillips, William Welsh, William Eugene.

It—1927. Famous Players–Lasky. *Distributor:* Paramount Pictures. Silent. B&W. 35mm. 7 reels, 6,452 feet. *Presented by:* Adolph Zukor, Jesse L. Lasky. *Associate Producer:* B.P. Schulberg. *Director:* Clarence Badger. *Additional Director:* Josef von Sternberg. *Scenario:* Hope Loring, Louis D. Lighton. *Title:* George Marion, Jr. *Adaptation:* Elinor Glyn. *Photographer:* H. Kinley Martin. *Editor in Chief:* Lloyd Sheldon. *Assistant Director:* Vernon Keays. *Cast:* Clara Bow, Antonio Moreno, William Austin, Jacqueline Gadsdon, Gary Cooper,

Julia Swayne Gordon, Priscilla Bonner, Eleanor Lawson, Rose Tapley, Elinor Glyn.

Long Pants—1927. Harry Langdon Corp. *Distributor:* First National Pictures. Silent. B&W. 35mm. 6 reels, 5,550 feet. *Director:* Frank Capra. *Adaptation:* Robert Eddy. *Story:* Arthur Ripley. *Photographer:* Elgin Lessley, Glenn Kershner. *Comedy Construction:* Clarence Hennecke. *Cast:* Harry Langdon, Gladys Brockwell, Al Roscoe, Alma Bennett, Frankie Darro, Priscilla Bonner.

Broadway After Midnight—1927. Krelbar Pictures. Silent. B&W. 35mm. 7 reels, 6,199 feet. *Presented by:* Sherman S. Krellberg. *Director:* Fred Windermere. *Scenario:* Adele Buffington. *Story:* Frederic Bartel. *Photography:* Charles Davis. *Cast:* Matthew Betz, Priscilla Bonner, Cullen Landis, Gareth Hughes, Ernest Hilliard, Barbara Tennant, William Turner, Hank Mann, Paul Weigel.

Golden Shackles—1928. Dallas M. Fitzgerald Productions. *Distributor:* Peerless Pictures. Silent. B&W. 35mm. 6 reels, 5,600 feet. *Director:* Dallas M. Fitzgerald. *Scenario:* Ada McQuillan, Gladys Gordon. *Title:* M.C. Dewar. *Story:* G. Marion Burton. *Photography:* Milton Moore. *Film Editor:* M.D. Dewar. *Cast:* Grant Withers, Priscilla Bonner, LeRoy Mason, Ruth Stewart.

Outcast Souls—1928. Sterling Pictures. Silent. B&W. 35mm. 6 reels, 4,866 feet. *Supervisor:* Joe Rock. *Director:* Louis Chaudet. *Scenario:* Jean Plannette. *Title:* H. Tipton Steck. *Adaptation/Story:* Norman Houston. *Photography:* Herbert Kirkpatrick. *Film Editor:* H. Tipton Steck. *Music:* Cues Michael Hoffman. *Cast:* Priscilla Bonner, Charles Delaney, Ralph Lewis, Lucy Beaumont, Tom O'Brien.

Girls Who Dare—1929. Trinity Pictures. Silent. B&W. 35mm. 6 reels, 5,400–5,600 feet. *Director:* Frank S. Mattison. *Scenario:* Cecil Burtis Hill. *Title:* Arthur Hotaling. *Story:* Frank S. Mattison, Ben Hershfield. *Photography:* Jules Cronjager. *Film Editor:* Minnie Steppler. *Cast:* Rex Lease, Priscilla Bonner, Rosemary Theby, Ben Wilson, Steve Hall, Eddie Brownell, Sarah Roberts, May Hotely, Hall Cline.

Virginia Cherrill

Virginia Cherrill was in ill health at the time we were finally able to set up a telephone interview. Miss Cherrill's longtime friend, Teresa McWilliams, and her secretary Carrie DeWitt arranged the interview but expressed real concern that I may have to call back due to Virginia's failing health. As it turned out, we were able to talk for some time before Miss Cherrill needed to hang up. This is, I believe, the last interview she granted and I am honored to include her here. Born on April 12, 1908, Miss Cherrill was 87 years old when we spoke.

"I'm sorry but the nurse was here. I haven't been very well. I fell and fractured my spine. I've been an invalid for ten years. I'm very fragile so you will have to forgive me if I don't go on too long. I'm having some eye surgery in the morning.

Virginia Cherrill had no driving ambition to be in movies, nor was it her desire to attain Olympian heights as an actress. She came out to Hollywood from her hometown of Carthage, Illinois, to see her school friend, Sue Carol, who *was* enjoying success in films. This was 1928. I asked her how she got her start in films and to please talk a bit about Charlie Chaplin. After all, she co-starred with him in *City Lights* (1931) when Chaplin was still unwilling to cross over into talking pictures. Of course he eventually relented but not before making his last silent film, *Modern Times*, in 1936.

"I fell in! I wasn't an actress. I was visiting my godmother in California and went to a prize fight in Los Angeles. I'd never been to a prize fight and I sat next to a little man with white hair, very tanned, a stranger.

"He kept *staring* at me. I didn't wear my glasses when I went out, so of course I didn't see. I was vain. Well, I was with a friend of the

Virginia Cherrill in 1932 (photograph by Kahle).

family, an elderly gentleman. The next day he called
me up and said, 'That was
Charlie Chaplin you sat
next to!'

"I said, 'Don't be silly!' I
mean to me, I thought Charlie had a little black hat and
baggy pants. 'No', he said, 'he
wants us to come to his beach
house for lunch. Would you
like to go?'

"So I went and Mr.
Chaplin ended up seeing
me. Mr. D'Arrast said,
'Charlie, that's the girl I've
been telling you about,' and
Charlie said, 'Oh no, that's
the girl I've been telling *you*
about!'"

What Virginia didn't
know at the moment was
that she had already been
spotted by director Harry
D'Arrast, who had told
Chaplin about her potential
screen quality. And by not
wearing her glasses, Vir-
ginia did herself the great-

Charlie Chaplin and Virginia Cherrill in *City Lights* (1931).

est favor she could have—to appear blind! Soon Chaplin would
be approaching her to play the blind girl in his now classic *City
Lights*.

In Chaplin's autobiography, he alludes to the fact that Virginia
approached *him* on Santa Monica Beach where she was supposedly with
an unnamed film company. "When am I going to work for you?" Virginia allegedly ask Chaplin. This simply is not factual. *City Lights* was
Cherrill's first film experience and it's been well documented she was
"discovered" at the prize fight. Furthermore, she *never* had a screen test
despite what some early publications indicate.

WORKING WITH CHAPLIN

"Harry D'Arrast was a [French] friend of Chaplin's. He later married Eleanor Boardman and Chaplin had brought him back from Paris to be advisor on the last film he did called *A Woman of Paris* [1923].

"Harry had evidently seen me at the Ambassador Hotel and thought I looked blind because I *peer* at people. So Charlie saw me at the prize fight but they didn't *know* I could see. That's how I got in. I never made a test, I never acted. Charlie said it was a good thing 'cause I would have had to unlearn everything I knew!

Chaplin with actress Lita Gray, later Mrs. Charlie Chaplin.

Society Girl: Pretty Virginia Cherrill, Cary Grant's first wife.

"It took *two* years to complete the film! He was always improvising and changing things."

When I asked Virginia if she thought she'd ever want to work again after *City Lights* she quickly and emphatically said, "No!"

But the film was a success and Virginia did indeed work again. When I spoke to her devoted friend, Teresa, she told of Virginia reminiscing about her early career with Chaplin and how much Virginia actually disliked him although acknowledging his genius. His artistic demands on Virginia were indeed extreme and sometimes unreasonable.

"Apparently Chaplin was somewhat of an egomanic. He would interrupt the filming *constantly* to go play tennis and Virginia got tired of hanging around the studio waiting. So one day when he returned and found her gone, he fired her."

After almost two years Chaplin still couldn't find a replacement as suitable as Virginia, whose friend, actress Marion Davies, urged her to return but *not* before she ask Chaplin to *double* her salary. Chaplin did indeed comply, and the film was finally able to be completed.

Chaplin admits in his autobiography how one scene with Virginia which lasts seventy seconds on the screen took five days of re-takes to get right. "This was not the girl's [Virginia's] fault, but partly my own, for I had worked myself into a neurotic state of wanting perfection. *City Lights* took more than a year to make."

AFTER CHAPLIN

Despite Chaplin's directional demands, Virginia went on to make more films with stars such as John Gilbert and a young John Wayne.

She married Cary Grant in 1934, although the marriage dissolved after a year. She recalled some highlights of her later career.

"Well ... I was never a major star. I really was in the last big silent picture. I made some very forgettable films! I made one with Humphrey Bogart but I was fired from it. He wasn't a very tall man and they made him wear these boots to make him look taller. He just looked so funny! I kept giggling and they fired me!"

Miss Cherrill was tired so we brought the interview to a close. I tried one other occasion to talk but she simply wasn't able to do so. She was always so kind to talk when she could and so thankful to still be remembered. Miss Cherrill was gracious and generous to me. When she passed away I remember thinking of this beautiful blonde society girl from Carthage, Illinois, who chanced into films but left us a legacy. Can we ask for more?

FILMOGRAPHY

City Lights—1931. Charles Chaplin Productions. *Distributor:* United Artists Corp. Production began December 27, 1928. Silent with music soundtrack (Western Electric Sound System). B&W. 9 reels. 87 min. *Director:* Charles Chaplin. *Assistant Directors:* Harry Crocker, Henry Bergman and Albert Austin. *Script:* Charles Chaplin. *Photography:* Rollie Totheroh, Gordon Pollock and [Mark Marklatt]. *Sets:* Charles D. Hall [Film Ed Charles Chaplin]. *Music Director:* Alfred Newman. *Music Composition:* Charles Chaplin. *Musical Arrangements:* Arthur Johnston [Press representative Carlyle Robinson]. *Cast:* Charlie Chaplin, Virginia Cherril, Florence Lee, Harry Myers, Allan Garcia, Hank Mann, [Eddie Baker], [Henry Bergman].

The Brat—1931. Fox Film Corp. John Ford Production. *Distributor:* Fox Film Corp. Sound. B&W. 6,000 feet. 60 or 67 min. Passed by the National Board of Review. *Director:* John Ford, *Dialogue Director:* William Collier, Sr. [*Assistant Directors:* Ed O'Fearna and Wingate Smith]. *Adaptation/Continuity/Dialogue:* S.N. Behrman and Sonya Levien. *Photography:* Joseph August. *Art Director:* Jack Schulze. [*Film editor:* Alex Troffey]. *Additional Recording:* Eugene Grossman. [*Music Manager:* Harry Leonhardt]. *Cast:* Sally O'Neil, Allan Dinehart, Frank Albertson, William Collier, Sr., Virginia

Cherrill, June Collyer, Farrell MacDonald, Mary Forbes, Albert Gran, Louise Mackintosh, Margaret Mann.

Girls Demand Excitement—1931. Fox Film Corp. Seymour Felix Production. *Distributor:* Fox Film Corp. B&W. 7 reels, 6,050 feet. 64 or 68 min. *Passed by* the National Board of Review. *Presented by:* Wm. Fox. *Associate Producer:* Ralph Block. *Director:* Seymour Felix. [*Assistant Director:* Edward Marin]. *Story/Adaptation/Dialogue:* Harlan Thompson. [*Writers:* Owen Davis, W. Robertson, Harry Sauber, Ray Harris and R. Medcraft]. *Photography:* Charles Clarke. *Sets:* Jack Schulze. *Film Editor:* Jack Murray. *Cost:* Sophie Wachner. *Sound Recording:* Eugene Grossman. *Cast:* Virginia Cherrill, John Wayne, Marguerite Churchill, Edward Nugent, Helen Jerome Eddy, Terrance Ray, Martha Sleeper, William Janney, Ralph Welles, George Irving, Winter Hall, Marion Byron, Emerson Treacy, Addie McPhail, Jerry Mandy, Ray Cooke, Carter Gibson.

Fast Workers—1933. Metro-Goldwyn-Mayer Corp. *Controlled by* Loew's, Inc. Tod Browning's Production. *Distributor:* Metro-Goldwyn-Mayer Distributing Corp. [Western Electric Sound System]. B&W. 7 reels. 66 min. *Passed by* the National Board of Review. *Director:* Tod Browning. *Assistant Director:* Cedric Gibbons. *Film Editor:* Ben Lewis. *Recording Director:* Douglas Shearer. [*Mixer:* Fred Morgan]. *Cast:* Virginia Cherrill, John Gilbert, Robert Armstrong, Mae Clarke, Muriel

Kirkland, Vince Barnett Holloway, Guy Usher, Warner Richmond, Robert Burns.

Charlie Chan's Greatest Case—1933. Fox Film Corp. *Distributor:* Fox Film Corp. Sound. B&W. 8 reels, 6,200 feet. 70–71 min. *Series:* Charlie Chan. *Producer:* Sol M. Wurtzel. *Director:* Hamilton MacFadden. *Assistant Director:* Percy Ikerd. *Script:* Lester Cole and Marion Orth. *Photography:* Ernest Palmer. *Assistant Camera:* Stanley Little and Robert Mack. *Sets:* Duncan Cramer, Ed Alex Troffey. *Gowns:* Royer. *Musical Cir:* Samuel Kaylin. *Sound:* George Leverett. *Assistant Sound:* W.T. Brent. *Still Photography:* Cliff Maupin. *Cast:* Warner Oland, Heather Angel, Roger Imhof, John Warburton, Walter Byron, Ivan Simpton, Virginia Cherrill, Francis Ford, Robert Warwick, Frank McGlynn, Clara Blandick, Claude King, William Stack, Gloria Roya, Cornelius Keefe.

He Couldn't Take It—1933. Monogram Pictures Corp. Trem Carr, Vice-President in Charge of Production. A W.T. Lackey Production. *Distributor:* Monogram Pictures Corp. Sound. B&W. 7 reels. 63, 65, or 68 min. *Passed by* National Board of Review. *Director:* William Nigh. *Script/Story:* Dore Schary. *Additional Dialogue:* George Waggner. *Photography:* Jack MacKenzie. *Sets:* E.R. Hickson, Ed Jack Ogilvie. *Recording:* John A. Stransky, Jr. *Cast:* Ray Walker, Virginia Cherrill, George E. Stone, Stanley Fields, Dorothy Granger, Paul Porcasi, Jane Darwell, Donald Douglas, Astrid Allwyn, Franklin Parker, Jack Kennedy, Florence Turner.

Ladies Must Love—1933. Universal Pictures Corp. *Distributor:* Universal Pictures Corp. Sound. B&W. 8 reels. 60 or 70–71 min. *Producer:* Carl Laemmle, Jr. *Director:* E.A. Dupont. *Assistant Director:* William Reiter. *Script:* John Frankis Larkin. *Contributing Writers:* William Hurlbut, Robert Harris, Harry Sauber, Carey Wilson, Fred Niblo, Jr., Richard Weil and Kerry Clarke. *Contributor to treatment:* Tom Kilpatrick. *Photography:* Tony Gaudio. *Camera Operator:* Richard Fryer. *Assistant Camera:* William Dodds. *Art Director:* Danny Hall. *Editor:* Robert Carlisle. *Sound Recording:* Gilbert Kurland. *Recording Engineer:* Fred Feichter. *Assistant Recording Engineer:* Vanneman. *Chief Electrician:* Irving Smith. *Chief Grip:* Fred Parkinson. *Props:* Harry Grundstrum. *Still Photography:* Shirley Vance. *Cast:* June Knight, Neil Hamilton, Sally O'Neil, Dorothy Burgess, Mary Carlisle, George E. Stone, Maude Eburne, Oscar Apfel, Edmund Breese, Richard Carle, Berton Churchill, Virginia Cherrill.

The Nuisance—1933. Metro-Goldwyn-Mayer Corp. *Controlled by* Loew's Inc. *Distributor:* Metro-Goldwyn Mayer Corp. Sound (Western Electric Sound System). B&W. 9 reels. 80–81 min. *Passed by* the National Board of Review. *Associate Producer:* Lawrence Weingarten. *Director:* Jack Conway. *Assistant Director:* Joseph Newman. *Original Story:* Chandler Sprague and Howard Emmett Rogers. *Adaptation and Dialogue:* Bella Spewack and Samuel Spewack. *Photography:* Gregg Toland. *Art Director:* Cedric Gibbons. *Film Editor:* Frank Sullivan. *Recording Director:* Douglas Shearer. *Cast:* Lee Tracy, Madge Evans, Frank Morgan, Charles Butterworth, John Miljan, Virginia Cherrill, David Landau, Greta Mayer, Herman Bing, Samuel Hinds, Syd Saylor, Nat Pendleton, Edgar Dearing.

White Heat—1934. Seven Seas Corp. *Distributor:* State Rights. Pinnacle Productions, Inc. Sound. B&W. 60–62 min. *Producer:* William Fiske, III. *Director:* Lois Weber. *Script:* Lois Weber. *Original Story/Script:* James Bordrero. *Photography:* Alvin Wyckoff and Frank Titus. *Music Supervisor:* Abe Meyer. *Cast:* Virginia Cherrill, Mona Maris, Hardie Albright, David Newell, Arthur Clayton, Robert Stevenson, Whitney de Rahm, Naomi Childers, Nani Palso, Kolimau Kamai, Kamaunani Achi, Peter Lee Hyun, Nohili Naumu.

What Price Crime?—1935. Beacon Productions, Inc. *Distributor:* State Rights. Sound. B&W. 63–65 min. *Producer:* Max Alexander. *Associate Producer:* Peter E. Kassler. *Director:* Albert Herman. *Story/Script:* Al Martin. *Photography:* Harry Forbes. *Editor:* S. Roy Luby. *Cast:* Charles Starrett, Noel Madison, Virginia Cherrill, Charles Delaney, Jack Mulhall, Nina Guilbert, Henry Roquemore, Gordon Griffith, John Elliot, Arthur Loft, Earl Tree, Jack Cowell, Arthur Rowlands, Edwin Argus, Al Baffert, Monte Carter, Laft McKee.

Pauline Curley

"My gosh, when you start to work when you are seven years old, why I think you deserve to quit at twenty four!" Pauline Curley was remembering her pioneering career in films. We had set up a telephone interview after she had sold her home in Calabasas, California. Now settled in a new residence, she agreed to talk about her remarkable career at age 94. Born December 19, 1903, in Holyoke, Massachusetts, Miss Curley recalled her remarkable past with relish.

Pauline wasn't exactly ecstatic to be in a new place. After all, she'd been in her home almost fifty years and with moving and all, she couldn't immediately locate all her movie materials from her career. Nonetheless, her memory served her well and she talked for an hour about the early days.

"I have a scrapbook and I was very surprised about over in England, one of my most popular pictures I made years ago called *Cassidy* is such a popular picture! I got this letter from a gentleman over there."

But how, I wondered, did a seven year old girl start a career in cinema? And particularly, prior to 1920? "It was definitely my mother! She started me in dancing school when I was three years old. Singing and dancing, and so by the time I was seven she decided I was ready for Broadway so we went to New York City to live. She started to go to different studios and then, we started to get work.

"So I started working in motion pictures when I was seven years old. By the time I was eight and nine I was really doing it real well! I was in every picture if they used a little girl. I started with [director] Allan Dwan when I was nine years old."

Pauline Curley as a young boy in *The Straight Road* (directed by Allan Dwan, 1913).

Pauline would have a long and fruitful relationship with Mr. Dwan who was both a good friend and supporter of her film career.

DIRECTOR ALLAN DWAN

"My mother took me to see Mr. Dwan when she knew he was going to start a new movie. She said, 'Mr. Dwan, do you have a part for Pauline in your new picture?' He said, 'No, we are going to have to use a boy.' So my mother said okay and immediately went running away next door to our neighbors who had boys, borrowed an outfit, dressed me up and took me back to Mr. Dwan.

"She said, 'Mr. Dwan, here's your boy,' and by golly, I got the part! I have a picture of [myself] dressed as a boy the way I was in the picture. That was in 1913 so I was just ten years old at that time.

"Yes, being with Mr. Dwan at eight and nine years old he knew me from a little girl and saw me grow up. I kind of felt maybe I was more like his daughter. His first wife's name was Pauline but he was divorced ... but it was Pauline!" Miss Curley chuckled.

"I thought, why did he always show so much interest in me and my career and everything? Ma and I were in the back waiting for me to be called to do a scene and Mr. Dwan came up and he had a little rock, a little stone in his hand and he said, 'Pauline, I am going to give you this now. And I am giving this to you that someday you will become a big star and have all the success in the world.'

"I never forgot it and I kept that for years and years and years! I thought it was kind of silly, I was just a little girl. I got rid of it but I often regretted it afterwards that I did, it was just awful."

Pauline recalled when at age eighteen, she eloped and married Kenneth Peach on May 2, 1922. She still was working with Mr. Dwan and he continued to look out for her career.

"I was running away! My husband and I had eloped. Mr. Dwan called me and said, 'Look Pauline, I know you remember Mickey [Marshall] Neilan and Blanche Sweet?' Well they were married at the time and Mr. Dwan said they were having a party at the Ambassador Hotel in the Coconut Grove. He said, 'Do you think your husband would let you go? After all, they would all be movie stars and directors.'

"Well I explained to my husband it would be good for my career to go out and meet people like that so he agreed. I went with Mr. Dwan to the Ambassador to the big party with Mr. Neilan and Blanche Sweet.

"And then, that one show with Mr. Dwan and Gloria Swanson was the star but I had a part in it. We went down to San Diego and stayed at the big hotel and the company had put me in with another lady. We shared a room and, oh! Mr. Dwan found out about that! 'Oh, no ... Pauline Curley has her *own* room!' Those are the things you never forget!"

VAUDEVILLE AND BROADWAY

As if Pauline Curley's career in films wasn't impressive enough, she also found herself touring in early vaudeville and on Broadway. All this training and exposure would serve Pauline well once she settled in Los Angeles, continuing a career which encompassed over forty films.

"My mother was ambitious for me and started me in dancing school. She decided to take me to New York so I could be an actress. When I was ten years old my mother and I were in a vaudeville act. We traveled all over the United States and Canada. *A Daddy by Express* was the name of the act.

"And then before that my mother and I were in summer stock in New Jersey. I played Eva in *Uncle Tom's Cabin* with Jack Packard's Stock Company and then also, *The Outlaw's Christmas*. But something funny happened with Eva in the finale!

"In the end of it, Eva's going to Heaven and so they had a backing of clouds that they put up in front of a ladder. My father came over on Saturday night to see the show. So I'm up on this ladder with my hands together, going to Heaven and the backing fell down and showed me standing on a ladder!

"Oh! I was humiliated thinking my father was out in front watching the show but everyone had to laugh! After I ended the vaudeville I came back to New York City and then went for an interview to play a part in a Broadway show called *Polygamy*.

"And so the only thing that would hold me up on that was that I was up on my studies. I had a private tutor who was teaching me what at that time was called the Phyfe system. I was up on my studies, I passed. I had to go to the board of education but I passed for my age and I got the part.

"I was a whole year in *Polygamy*. Well by the time I was twelve years old, my mother said, 'Now I don't know what we are going to do with you. The only thing we can do is put you in long dresses.' And that is exactly what she did.

As fair as the rose she's holding: Pauline Curley in 1919 (photo by Evans).

"So I started as they called it in those days, as an ingenue. I went to professional children's school. We worked 'til eleven every night in the show so I didn't get home and in bed until midnight and then you don't have to be to school until ten the next morning. After all, the children were in plays and things.

"Then on Wednesday you have a matinee so they let you leave at noon so you have a break for the two o'clock matinee. I have had the experience not only in pictures but in stock companies, vaudeville and Broadway shows."

Harold Lockwood

Pauline Curley worked a lot in films on the East Coast. Between New York and New Jersey, she was featured with such companies as Biograph, Triangle and Mutual. Looking older than her twelve years and with the help of her mother, she convinced director Fred Balshofer that she was ready for "adult" roles.

Balshofer was producer and director to silent star Harold Lockwood, and he and Pauline would become successful partners in film and good friends as well.

"I was never around children and when I was young, I was working so I was with adults, always with adults. When you work when you are seven years old, you don't play. So actually when I starred with Harold Lockwood I was just fourteen years old but I didn't *feel* fourteen. I felt like I was much older.

"Well Harold took a liking to me after all so he said, 'Why don't you come with me in the morning in my limousine to the [film] location?' I said, 'Oh that would be wonderful!' So I went with him in his limousine and then for lunch together. His company would have lunch wherever they were working.

"Well this went on for just a little while and then all at once he didn't ask me to go with him anymore in his limousine! So I said to my mother, 'You know, I don't understand. Harold always took me to the location in his limousine.'

"She said, 'I'll tell you why. I showed him your birth certificate!' That took care of that. Then he treated me like a little girl! That actually happened!

"If I got home from work early I'd go out with the kids and play Run Shake Run and Hide and Seek out in the road. Here I'm out there sweating, having fun and who drives up in his Marvin, Harold Lockwood and his girlfriend! I thought, 'Oh wait 'til he sees me!'

"He *had* to see me, I had to go over to him. He laughed and said, 'My leading lady! Look at my leading lady playing like a little girl!' But it was true.

"I was really only thirteen years old to start as a leading lady. Mr. Balshofer thought I was sixteen but actually I started in December with Harold Lockwood and I wasn't fourteen until the nineteenth. It was a wonderful opportunity for me and so I did a show with him and then I went to Florida with another company and did a show called *His Boy*.

"Then I came back and they wanted me with Harold Lockwood again and we went back to Florida and did a picture show there called *The Landloper* [1918]. That's when Mr. Balshofer's office called and said, 'Mrs. Curley, I would like to have you and Pauline come to California and continue working with Harold.' That was 1918 [when] I came out to Hollywood."

Looking back on making films with Harold Lockwood, Pauline's genuine affection is obvious. "I felt very bad when he died because I definitely liked him not only as an actor to work with but I thought he was real nice as a man." More adventures, however, lay ahead once she arrived in Hollywood in 1918.

HOLLYWOOD 1918

Pauline's success with Harold Lockwood was assured. Now establishing herself as a fine screen actress, soon another Hollywood great, director King Vidor, would be important to her career.

"King Vidor was going to make his very first [feature] film, *The Turn in the Road* [1919]. Now one of my pictures had been shown at the Broadway Theater in Los Angeles. It was one of the biggest theaters. We knew the owner, P.T. Tally, and so King Vidor went to him for advice.

"He said, 'I suggest that you get Pauline Curley in your picture, it would help sell it.' So I got the part. King Vidor was a Christian scientist and a very, very nice man. Lloyd Hughes was his first discovery and he played my husband in that."

Prior to this film, Pauline had an opportunity to work with Douglas Fairbanks in *Bound for Morocco* (1919). The film was directed by Allan Dwan. Of Fairbanks, Pauline remembers him as "very nice." "After all, he knew Mr. Dwan was directing, he knew I was young."

She knew Fairbanks' wife too. Mary Pickford, "America's Sweetheart," met Pauline when she was working at Famous Players with Allan Dwan. Like Pauline's mother who was seldom separated from her daughter, so too was Mary's mother, Charlotte.

"Her mother Charlotte was *always* with her, even *after* she was married. It didn't make any difference." Pauline would soon be asking her mother to allow *her* more freedom. Unlike Charlotte Pickford, Mrs. Curley would comply.

"As I told you before, my mother was always with me. Well when I was working at Vitagraph with Antonio Moreno, my mother was still

Actor Antonio Moreno with his director William Bowman (circa 1918).

going to the studio with me. They made a caricature of my mother and me and then here's the big mother and I am the little Pauline holding her hand! It was embarrassing to me that I had to hold my mother's hand to work.

"So I showed it to my mother and I said, 'Mom, we just can't go on doing this anymore. I am sixteen years old. I am going to work by myself from now on.' She agreed it was right so I went to work by myself. Before that, she was always with me but when they started to make fun of me about it, that was too much!

A Date with Jack

By now, Pauline was working all the time and meeting lots of new people. She recalled working with one of early Hollywood's biggest stars, John Gilbert.

"We made a picture together called *The Man Beneath* [1919]. He was the juvenile, I was the ingenue and Sessue Hayakawa, remember that name? Helen Jerome Eddy was in that show too.

"Anyway Jack, as we called him, said, 'Any chance you will be able to go out and have dinner with me down at the Athletic Club?' which was the most popular place for movie stars and directors at the time. I said, 'I don't know. I'll have to talk to my mother about it.' After all, I wasn't allowed to date.

"And so I asked her. I said, 'Mama, you know after all there will be a lot of big people there, producers, stars and everything.' She said, 'Well all right. I'll let you go *once*.' And so I went. I *did* have a date with John Gilbert!' Pauline laughed.

And what about Gilbert's romance with Garbo? "Well that would be later. After all, I was married then but he made quite a few pictures with her you know."

BIG NAMES AND BIG TIMES

Probably in retrospect, Hollywood in the twenties was no different than today. Sex, bootleg booze, drugs and scandal all made for a good headline. Pauline recalled in particular the Roscoe "Fatty" Arbuckle ordeal.

"By that time I was married and twenty three years old. I thought [the Arbuckle scandal] was sort of a disgrace for the motion picture business. That was my feeling about it. I never heard of anything like that. It was difficult for Hollywood, there's no doubt about that.

"It was a very unfortunate thing that happened. It was up in San Francisco. They had this big party. I guess they had too much to drink. He did something he shouldn't have, that was all. He was one of my favorite comedians. It just seemed a shame to get involved in something like that and lose your career.

"I thought Valentino was a good actor. It was very sad when he died but I never cared about the Latin types. Of course he was a big star but I didn't know anything about him.

"The longest I worked was at Vitagraph with Antonio Moreno. I worked there two years and we got along just fine. When you work together for two years you become well acquainted. I went from Antonio Moreno and did a show with Tom Mix.

"I made a whole series of comedies and westerns with Jack Perrin and Bobby Ray. I alternated; I did a western and then make a comedy with Bobby Ray. The other comedian was Al [Alexander] Alt. He was the star and Bobby Ray directed. When Bobby was the star, we always had an outside director come in. I worked all the time."

THE REGULARS

Pauline Curley did indeed work all the time. Cranking out film after film probably left little time for socializing. There was, however, a group of leading ladies who met every week just for fun. Organized by Pauline, they were soon known as "The Regulars."

"You had to be a leading lady to join. Virginia [Brown Faire] and I were the ones who organized the club. Priscilla [Bonner] and her

"The Regulars." *Back row, left to right:* **Marion Nixon, Duane Thompson, Marjorie Bonner, Menifee Johnstone, Virginia Brown Faire, Dorothy Devore, and Lucille Hutton.** *First row, left to right:* **Priscilla Bonner, Maryon Aye, Mary Philbin, Pauline Curley, Grace Gordon, and Pauline Garon,** April 1924 (courtesy of Pauline Curley).

Top: Gloria Swanson. *Bottom:* Priscilla Bonner.

sister Margie, she was in it too. We met every Monday night and discussed what we'd been doing and so forth.

"There was a girl, her name was Maryon Aye [in the group]. She committed suicide. I could never understand why, you know, why she committed suicide. She was a young girl."

The *Los Angeles Times* carried a photo and article on "The Regular Fellows' Club" April 29, 1924. It mentions the girls making strawberry shortcake and Grace Gordon giving Mary Philbin a manicure. "The official cooks for the evening were Maryon Aye and Pauline Garon."

The members included Maryon Aye, Priscilla and Marjorie Bonner, Pauline Curley, Dorothy Devore, Virginia Brown Faire, Pauline Garon, Grace Gordon, Lucille Hutton, Menifee Johnstone, Marion Nixon, Mary Philbin and Duane Thompson. The article's title aptly sums it up: "Acting for Films Not Everything in Their Young Lives."

MOVING ON

Pauline would eventually meet and fall in love with Kenneth Peach. Not willing to endure the resistance of her mother, Pauline and Ken eloped on May 2, 1922. Pauline was only eighteen.

Ken started in films also—at the Special Effects Department at Paramount with Roy Pomeroy. "I didn't get pregnant for eight years so when I did, then I told my husband, 'I'm through, I'm not going to work anymore.' I thought working from seven years old to twenty four, that's enough."

Pauline had her first child, a son, in 1930. Kenneth, Jr., would be joined by a sister Pauline, in 1935, and another brother, Marty, in 1949. Pauline was then forty-five.

"I didn't have Marty until I was forty five years old. What a big surprise that was in our family! But I would tell anyone, don't ever be disappointed and say, 'Oh, this is awful having children late in life.' It was wonderful because my two older children, they married young and left and we had our Marty home with us. So I tell anyone, don't be upset if they get pregnant late in life because it's beautiful, it really is."

LIFE TODAY

Pauline Curley will be ninety-five when this book is published. She is witty, intelligent and loves to recall her career in cinema. She continues to receive fan mail and requests for photos from all over the world.

"I have lots of fans. I have fans in England! You see, there's not many people left. They're all dead. Another thing I am very proud of, I am in the Library of Congress. I made forty-one films altogether you know.

"The New York Public Library has everything about me. Go in there and ask for Pauline Curley."

I thanked Miss Curley and ask her how she'd like to be remembered. She laughed lightly.

"I would like to be remembered as a good child actress and leading lady." I assured her that forty-one films later and despite the fading of those glorious early Hollywood days, she would indeed inspire, entertain and educate future generations.

FILMOGRAPHY

Life Without Soul—1915. Ocean Film Corp. *Distributor:* State Rights. 5 reels. *Director:* Joseph W. Smiley. *Scenario:* Jesse J. Goldburg. *Source:* Based on the novel *Frankenstein* by Mary W. Shelley (London, 1818). *Cast:* William W. Cohill, Percy Darrell Standing, George De Carlton, Lucy Cotton, Pauline Curley, Jack Hopkins, David McCauley, Violte De Biccari.

The Unbroken Road—1915. Life Photo Film Corp. *Writing Credits:* Thomas W. Dickinson. *Cast:* James Ayres, Joseph Baker, Sue Balfour, Pauline Curley, Nellie Dent, Frank DuFrane, Alexander Gaden, Charles Graham, Walter James, Arthur Morrison, Thomas O'Keefe, Edna Spence, William H. Tooker.

The Girl Philippa—1916. *Writing Credits:* Robert W. Chambers. *Director:* S. Rankin Drew. Vitagraph Co. of America. *Cast:* Pauline Curley, S. Rankin Drew, Frank Morgan, Anders Randolf, Anita Stewart.

Cassidy—1917. Triangle Film Corp. *Distributor:* Triangle Distributing Corp. 5 reels. *Director:* Arthur Rosson. Cam Roy Overbaugh. *Cast:* Pauline Curley, Dick Rosson, Frank Currier, Mac Alexander, Eddie Sturgis, John O'Connor, Jack Snyder.

The Square Deceiver—1917. Yorke Film Corp. *Distributor:* Metro Pictures Corp. A Metro Wonderplay. Metro Pictures Corp. 5 reels. *Direc-tor:* Fred J. Balshofer. *Scenario:* Fred J. Balshofer and Richard V. Spencer. *Camera:* Antonio Gaudio. *Cast:* Harold Lockwood, Pauline Curley, William Clifford, Dora Mills Adams, Kathryn Hutchinson, Betty Marvin, Dick L'Estrange.

The Fall of the Romanoffs—1917. (Also known as **The Downfall of the Romanoffs**) *Writing Credits:* George Edwardes-Hall, Austin Strong. *Director:* Herbert Brenon. *Producers:* Herbert Brenon, Iliodor Pictures Corp. *Distributor:* First National Exhibitors Circuit. *Cast:* Peter Barbierre, W. Francis Chapin, Edward Connelly, Charles Craig, Pauline Curley, Georges Deneubourg, Ketty Galanta, Robert Paton Gibbs, Alfred Hickman, Iliodor, Sonia Marcelle, Nance O'Neil, Paul Porcasi, Charles Edward Russell, William E. Shay, Conway Tearle.

A Case at Law—1917. *Director:* Arthur Rosson. *Writing Credits:* William Dudley Pelley. *Cinematography:* Roy F. Overbaugh, Allan Dwan, supervisor. Triangle Film Corp. *Cast:* Richard Rosson, Pauline Curley, Riley Hatch, John T. Dillon, Eddie Sturgis.

Mr. Fix-It—1918. *Art Craft:* Paramount Pictures (Douglas Fairbanks Pictures). *Producer:* Douglas Fairbanks. *Cinematography:* Hugh McClung. *Writing Credits:* Ernest Butterworth, Allan Dwan, Joseph Henabery. *Cast:* Douglas Fairbanks, Wanda Hawley, Marjorie

Daw, Frank Campeau, Pauline
Curley, Katherine MacDonald,
Leslie Stuart, Ida Waterman, Alice
H. Smith, Mrs. H.R. Hancock,
Mr. Russell, Fred Goodwins, Margaret Landis, Jack Pickford.

Lend Me Your Name—1918. Yorke
Film Corp. *Distributors:* Metro
Pictures Corp., All-Star Series.
Metro Pictures Corp. 5 reels.
Director: Fred J. Balshofer. *Scenario:* Fred J. Balshofer and John
B. Clymer. *Camera:* Antonio Gaudio. *Cast:* Harold Lockwood,
Pauline Curley, Bessie Eyton, Bert
Starkey, Stanton Heck, Peggy Prevost, Harry DeRoy.

Her Boy—1918. Metro Pictures
Corp. Metro All Star Series. Metro
Pictures Corp. 5 reels. *Supervisor:*
Maxwell Karger. *Director:* George
Irving. *Assistant Director:* Leander
DeCordova. *Scenario:* Albert
Shelby Le Vino. *Camera:* Harry B.
Harris. *Cast:* Effie Shannon, Niles
Welch, Pauline Curley, James T.
Galloway, Charles W. Sutton,
Charles Riegel, Violet Axzell,
Robert Chandler, Ferike Boros,
Anthony Byrd, S. McAlpin, J.C.
Bates, Edmund Wright, George F.
Demarest.

The Landloper—1918. Yorke Film
Corp. *Distributor:* Metro Pictures
Corp., All-Star Series. Metro Pictures Corp. 5 reels. *Director:*
George Irving. *Scenario:* John B.
Clymer. *Adaptation:* Fred J. Balshofer. *Camera:* Antonio Gaudio.
Cast: Harold Lockwood, Pauline
Curley, Staton Heck, William
Clifford, Bert Starkey, Gertrude
Maloney.

Bound in Morocco—1918. Douglas
Fairbanks Pictures Corp. *Distributor:* Famous Players–Lasky Corp.,

Artcraft Pictures. Douglas Fairbanks Pictures Corp. 5 reels. *Director:* Allan Dwan. *Scenario:* Allan
Dwan. *Camera:* Hugh McClung.
Cast: Douglas Fairbanks, Pauline
Curley, Edythe Chapman, Tully
Marshall, Frank Campeau, Jay
Dwiggins, Fred Burns, Albert
McQuarrie.

The Solitary Sin—1919. New Art
Film Co. *Distributor:* Solitary Sin
Corp. 6 reels. *Presented by:* George
D. Watters. *Supervisor:* George D.
Watters. *Director:* Frederick Sullivan. *Scenario:* George D. Watters.
Story: George D. Watters. *Camera:*
King D. Gray. *Cast:* Jack Mulhall,
Helene Chadwick, Gordon
Griffith, Pauline Curley, Anne
Schaefer, Irene Aldwyn, Leo Pierson, Charles Spere, Edward Jobson, Kate Lester, Berry Mills,
Edward Cecil, Milla Davenport,
Dorothea Wolbert.

The Man Beneath—1919. Haworth
Pictures Corp. *Distributor:* Robertson-Cole Co. through Exhibitors
Mutual Distributing Corp. The
Haworth Pictures Corp. 5 reels.
Director: William Worthington.
Scenario: L.V. Jefferson. *Camera:*
Frank D. Williams. *Technical
Director:* Frank D. Ormstrom. *Cast:*
Sessue Hayakawa, Helen Jerome
Eddy, Pauline Curley, Jack
Gilbert, Fountain La Rue, Wedgewood Nowell.

Hands Off—1921. Fox Film Corp.
Silent. B&W. 35mm. 5 reels, 4,158
feet. *Presented by:* William Fox.
Director: George E. Marshall. *Scenario:* Frank Howard Clark. *Story:*
William MacLeod Raine. *Photography:* Ben Kline. *Cast:* Tom Mix,
Pauline Curley, Charles K. French,
Frank Clark, Sid Jordan, William

McCormick, Sid Jordan, Virginia Warwick, J. Webster Dill, Marvin Loback.

The Turn in the Road—1919. *Writing:* King Vidor. *Director:* King Vidor. *Cast:* George Nicholls, Helen Jerome Eddy, Lloyd Hughes, Pauline Curley, Winter Hall, Ben Alexander.

The Veiled Mystery—1920. Vitagraph Co. of America. *Writing Credits:* C. Graham Baker, Cyrus Townsend Brady, Albert E. Smith. *Directors:* William Bowman, Webster Cullison, Francis J. Grandon, Antonio Moreno. *Cast:* Antonio Moreno, Pauline Curley, Henry A. Barrows, Nenette de Courcy, W.L. Rogers, George Reed, George Cooper, Valerio Olivo, Frank Lackteen.

The Invisible Hand—1920. Vitagraph Co. of America. *Director:* William Bowman. *Writing Credits:* C. Graham Baker, Cyrus Townsend Brady, Albert E. Smith. *Cast:* Antonio Moreno, Pauline Curley, Brinsley Shaw, Jay Morley, Sam Polo, George Mellcrest, Charles Rich II, Gordon Sackville. 15 episodes. First: 3 reels; rest 2 reels each.

Judge Her Not—1921. Harmony Film Co. *Distributor:* Sunnywest Films. Silent. B&W. 35mm (Feature Length assumed). *Director:* Scen George Edward Hall. *Cast:* Jack Livingston, Pauline Curley.

The Prairie Mystery—1922. Bud Osborne Feature Films. *Distributor:* TruArt Film Corp. Silent. B&W. 35mm. 5 reels. *Director/Writer:* George Edward Hall. *Cast:* Bud Osborne, Pauline Curley.

Midnight Secrets—1924. Robert J. Horner Productions. *Distributor:* RayArt Pictures. Silent. B&W.

35mm. 5 reels, 4,313 feet. *Director:* Jack Nelson. *Photography:* Jack Wilson. *Cast:* George Larkin, Ollie Kirby, Pauline Curley, Jack Richardson.

Shackles of Fear—1924. J. J. Fleming Productions. *Distributor:* Davis Distributing Division. Silent. B&W. 35mm. 5 reels, 4,416 feet. *Director:* Al Ferguson. *Cast:* Al Ferguson, Pauline Curley, Fred Dayton, Les Bate, Frank Clark, Bert De Vore, Paul Emery.

The Trail of Vengeance—1924. J.J. Fleming Productions. *Distributor:* Davis Distributing Division. Silent. B&W 35mm. 6 reels, 5,404 feet. *Director:* Al Ferguson. *Cast:* Al Ferguson, Pauline Curley.

His Greatest Battle—1925. Robert J. Horner Productions. *Distributor:* Aywon Film Corp. Silent. B&W. 35 mm. 5 reels, 4,900 feet. *Presented by:* Nathan Hirsh. *Director:* Robert J. Horner. *Cast:* Jack Randall, Kit Carson, Jack Richardson, Pauline Curley, John Pringle, Gladys Moore, Louis Moniago.

Cowboy Courage—1925. Robert J. Horner Productions. *Distributor:* Aywon Film Corp. Silent. B&W. 35mm. 5 reels, 4,800 feet. *Presented by:* Nathan Hirsh. *Director:* Leon De La Mothe. *Story/Continuity:* Robert J. Horner, Matilda Smith. *Photography:* Virgil Miller, Lauren A. Draper. *Cast:* Kit Carson, Pauline Curley, Jack Richardson, Walter Maly, C.L. James.

Twin Six O'Brien—1926. Robert J. Horner Productions. *Distributor:* Aywon Film Corp. Silent. B&W. 35mm. 5 reels. *Director:* Robert J. Horner. *Photography:* Lauren A. Draper. *Cast:* Kit Carson, Pauline Curley.

Pony Express Rider—1926. Robert J. Horner Productions. *Distributor:* Aywon Film Corp. Silent. B&W. 35mm. 5 reels, 4,750 feet. *Director:* Robert J. Horner. *Photography:* Lauren A. Draper. *Cast:* Kit Carson, Pauline Curley.

The Millionaire Orphan—1926. Fred Balshofer Productions. Silent. B&W. 35mm. 5 reels. *Director/ Writer:* Robert J. Horner. *Cast:* William Barrymore, Jack Richardson, Hal Ferner, Pauline Curley, Rex McIllvaine.

West of the Rainbow's End—1926. George Blaisdell Productions. *Distributor:* RayArt Pictures. Silent. B&W. 35mm. 5 reels, 4,829 feet. Harry Webb Production. *Director:* Bennett Cohn. *Scenario:* Daisy Kent. *Story:* Victor Rousseau. *Photography:* William Thornley. *Cast:* Jack Perrin, Pauline Curley, Billy Lamar, Tom London, James Welch, Milburn Morante, Whitehorse, Straight (a horse), Rex (a dog).

Walloping Kid—1926. Robert J. Horner Productions. *Director:* Robert J. Horner. *Writing Credits:* Robert J. Horner. *Cinematography:* Bert Baldridge. *Cast:* Kit Carson, Jack Richardson, Dorothy Ward, Frank Whitson, Al Kaufman, Jack Herrick, Pauline Curley.

Thunderbolt's Tracks—1927. Morris R. Schlank Productions. *Distributor:* RayArt Pictures. Silent. B&W. 35mm. 5 reels, 4,846 feet. *Director:* J.P. McGowan, Bennett Cohn. *Scenario:* Bennett Cohn. *Photography:* William Hyer. *Cast:* Jack Perrin, Pauline Curley, Jack Henderson, Billy Lamar, Ethan Laidlaw, Ruth Royce, Starlight (a horse).

Code of the Range—1927. Morris R. Schlank Productions. *Distributor:* RayArt Pictures. Silent. B&W. 35mm. 5 reels, 4,747 feet. *Presented by:* W. Ray Johnston. *Directors:* Bennett Cohn, Morris R. Schlank. *Cast:* Jack Perrin, Nelson McDowell, Pauline Curley, Lew Meehan, Chic Olsen, Starlight, Rex.

Power—1928. Pathé Exchange Inc. Distributors. *Director:* Howard Higgin. *Writing Credits:* Tay Garnett, John W. Krafft. *Producer:* Ralph Block. *Cinematography:* J. Peverell Marley. *Editing:* Doane Harrison, Robert Fellows. *Assistant Director:* Mitchell Leisen. *Art Directors:* Harry Poppe, Production Manager. *Cast:* William Boyd, Alan Hale, Jacqueline Logan, Jerry Drew, Joan Bennett, Carol Lombard, Pauline Curley.

Devil Dogs—1928. Morris R. Schlank Productions. *Distributor:* Anchor Film Distributors. Crescent Pictures. Silent. B&W. 35mm. 6 reels, 5,361 feet. *Director:* Fred Windermere. *Continuity:* Maxine Alton, Titl Al Martin. *Adaptation:* Adele Buffington. *Photography:* Robert E. Cline. *Film Editor:* L. Rosen. *Cast:* Alexander Alt, Pauline Curley, Stuart Holmes, Ernest Hilliard, J.P. McGowan.

The Locked Door—1929. Production Co. Feature Productions. *Distributor:* United Artists, Western Electric Sound System. *Director:* George Fitzmaurice *Producer:* George Fitzmaurice. *Cinematography:* Ray June, *Film Editing:* Hal C. Kern. *Dialogue:* Earle Browne, Joseph P. Kennedy. *Presenter:* Oscar Lagerstrom. *Monitor man:* William Cameron Menzies. *Art Director:* Robert H. Planck. *Assistant Cam-*

era: Cullen Tate. *Assistant Director/Writing Credits:* Earle Browne, Channing Pollock, George Scarborough, C. Gardner Sullivan. *Cast:* Rod La Rocque, Barbara Stanwick, William Stage Boyd, Betty Bronson, Harry Stubbs, Harry Mestayer, Mack Swain, ZaSu Pitts, George Bunny, Purnell Pratt, Fred Warren, Mary Ashcraft, Violet Bird, Earle Browne, Clarence Burton, Lita Chevret, Gilbert Clayton, Pauline Curley, Edgar Dearing, Edward Dillon, K. English, Eleanor Fredericks, Dorothy Gowan, Leona Leih, Virginia McFadden, Fletcher Norton, Robert Schable, Martha Stewart, Charles Sullivan, Greta von Rue.

Jean Darling

"I will talk to you if you do not use the information that is in the *Our Gang* book because so many things are wrong!"

Having not read the book she referred to, I assured Miss Darling that while I had only recently been aware of it, indeed I had to plead ignorance regarding its contents. A person deeply concerned with accuracy, she expressed frustration at times where misinformation or outright lies made up a passage on her life.

"I had an interview once and said I had been sick for a long time. The interviewer said, 'You never took sleeping pills or anything like that?' I said no, because I don't like the feeling of slipping away from myself the way I did when I was so sick. So it came out in the newspaper that I had given up drinking and drugs! That's what I mean," laughed Miss Darling. "I haven't figured it out yet why the man who wrote it is now doing a religious program which I think is rather sweet. You know, let's all fall down and pray to God because I am so truthful!"

Jean Darling has one of the most expressive, funny and delightful personas to interview. I had requested many times a telephone interview from her home in Dublin, Ireland, but all requests went unanswered. "I thought I would let you know.... I found you were persistent so I finally said yes."

NOT EVEN A YEAR OLD!

"Well, my father didn't want me to go into films. My mother said she was going to put on my little bonnet. I was five months old, my

God, I had been lying around for five months doing nothing! All I was doing was living off her.

"I'm third generation. My grandfather was in show business and my mother. So she was going to take me to central casting. My father said, 'Well if you want to put her in the movies, I won't be here when you get back.' Well Mamma said, 'ha ha' and off she went with me and when we came home, he was gone.

"I had some pictures taken and she registered me with central casting so I freelanced for awhile and I was in New York in a couple of plays with my mother. I was carried on stage and pinched to make me cry!

"Mamma's entire ambition was to get me in Our Gang while I was still freelancing in movies. So we moved into the Hunt Hotel and she camped on the doorstep of the Hal Roach Studio but that didn't do a bit of good. I was too young. They didn't want any little rats like me. You see she started camping out when I was about three.

"Then here was an article in the *Hollywood Citizen News* saying that they were having an open test for kids across the railroad tracks from Culver City. Of course she grabbed me by the paw and off we went flying!

"On the way we stopped in a chocolate shop to buy some sweets. In the shop was Mrs. Lloyd French, whom I proceeded to climb. Lloyd French was the vice president or something of Hal Roach Studio, I don't remember.

"When I got halfway up, my mother noticed and started to take me down. Mrs. French said, 'Oh don't bother, she is a lovely child,' which always makes mothers mad when they are trying to make a child behave, you know. So Mrs. French gave Mamma her card and she said to take me over to the Palms where they are making tests for Our Gang. Of course Mamma was very surprised that anything like tests were happening and thanked Mrs. French for the card. Off we went and I tested and got in the Gang. I was almost four."

Mr. Roach and the Gang

"Mr. Roach was a very nice man, at least he was nice to me. He gave us lovely Christmases. We had big parties on the set but you must realize that everybody I knew then, when I was a little tiny kid, was either nice or not nice.

Joe Cobb, Harry Spear, Allen "Farina" Hoskins, Jean Darling, Mary Ann Jackson, Bobby "Wheezer" Hutchins and Pete.

"Laurel and Hardy or Charlie Chase or when we went to MGM and knew Gable ... were like the butcher, the baker or candlestick maker. You don't say, 'Ahhhh, that's Clark Gable the star,' you just think, 'Oh, isn't he nice and cuddly and wouldn't he make a nice daddy.'

"I like Joe Cobb, the fat boy, very much. He and his father were nice people. His mother had died. Joe is still alive but he didn't grow very much taller. During the war he worked in an airplane factory. He could fit in places in the airplanes where ordinary size people couldn't.

"Harry Spear was the low point in my life. We were in vaudeville and doing a war scene, World War I. I was the nurse and they were all dressed as soldiers. He was carried in wounded from the battlefield and laid down on a stretcher in front of me. As a nurse, I took a huge light bulb to take his temperature.

"Harry very sweetly sticks his fingers up his nose, pulls out what's there, rolls it into a ball! This is all very quick, we're on the stage at the

Capitol Theatre in New York and he's rolling this thing up and he looks up at me as I am approaching him with the light bulb and says, 'Want a booger?!'

"So I jammed the light bulb in his mouth, very, very hard. This did *not* go over well with our keepers! I mean that's the kind of thing Harry did.

"Petey, Pete the dog, was nice because he got punished so he understood when *I* got punished and he would come over and commiserate with me! In the Our Gang book, they call him Pete the pup. Now, they might have done that in the forties long after I left the Gang but Petey came into the Gang when I was there.

"Pete the dog was born with a partial ring around his eye, about three quarters of the way around. Petey's trainer painted it the rest of the way around his eye, and he became 'Pete the dog with the ring around his eye.' This was the way he was advertised in all the sections across the country.

Hail! Hail! The Gang's All Here!

Our Gang members: Farina, Pete the dog and Joe.

"Mary Ann Jackson drove me crazy! She was a very cute looking and talented little thing but she drove me absolutely *nuts* because she was *always* playing jacks and eating sen sen for some reason. Aside from that I liked her.

"Her mother drove my mother crazy because she was a beautiful outgoing woman, and *my* mother was just beautiful. You see, Mary Ann Jackson's mother was a human being and my mother was a lady. Mrs. Jackson did not sit particularly well with Mamma. I don't think Mamma set very well with her either because they were such opposites.

"I liked Farina's mother. She was lovely and so nice. At the studio at that time there was a lot of jealousy of course, between parents. And particularly in Our Gang which was run as sort of a stock company.

"One picture would feature Joe, the next one might feature Farina and the next one might be built around Wheezer. Or it might be Pete who was the main character in the two reelers. There was always this jealousy between the parents. Naturally because there were *thousands* of kids out there whose parents were people who had failed in their own careers. Parents who tried to push their children into being stars so they could enjoy a bit of the limelight, a kind of peripheral stardom.

"The perimeter is lovely place to be because if you have a child who is a star, you become a star *immediately* because it's 'Mrs. Darling' on the set with Jean. And 'Oh, Mrs. Darling, publicity shots with Jean....' Of course Mrs. Darling is hovering in the background.

"An actress before I was born, mother was playing second leads. And she decided she was getting old so she had a face lift when she was twenty-six! That delighted me because everytime I got mad at her, I would lift up the little pancake braids she wore over each ear and shout, 'Look at Mamma's hem stitching!' She evidently had gone to someone who wasn't very good because he sewed the lobes of her ears in and there were little white lines around the bottom of her ears.

"We were supposed to have four hours in school every day. But what do you do with this little girl while school is in session, when instead of taking a nap she is bugging everybody? If you are Joe or Farina you teach her to read and write of course! Mrs. [Fern] Carter, the Our Gang tutor on the set, wasn't particularly interested in teaching me anything until I was older.

"When Farina came in the Gang as a baby, everyone thought he was a little girl because he wore little dresses. As he grew older they, of course, put him in pants. We use to have kids visit from Europe and they wore little smocks, you couldn't tell the boys from the girls unless you turned them upside down.

"Farina's sister was in the Gang for two or three movies. She was a little tiny girl and they brought her in because she was so cute. I remember her going around biting people and that sort of ended her career. People don't like being bit. I didn't think of biting her back. Besides, people were watching me!

A Sad Sign of the Times

"I met Harold Lloyd. He had been in partnership with Hal Roach making pictures. Then they had a falling out. One of the reasons they fell out was Our Gang. It first came out in 1919 as an idea that Roach had. It failed after three pictures and there was evidently a lot of contention between Harold Lloyd and Hal Roach.

"They eventually split up the partership and then in 1922, Hal Roach produced Our Gang again, and this time it lasted. The reason the Gang failed the first time was because there was a little black kid in it.

"A black child playing with children; this was *not* a good idea when you're trying to sell shorts in the southern part of the United States. Trying to book them in theaters and there's no way to *know* who this black child is. When the comedies came out the second time, there was a black man chopping wood or something. The black child was *his* and that excused it. It was all right for them to play together *if* the black one was the servant.

"It was just the way things were at the time, a sign of the times. Harold Lloyd use to come out to the lot occasionally. They still would have had a certain amount of business together because they had made so many pictures together. They would probably be rebooking them in theaters. Hal Roach shorts were released by Pathé when I first went on the lot and then we went over to MGM."

Our Little Rascals

Miss Darling told of how Our Gang later became Our Little Rascals. She also explained why the earlier silent films played much better and made more "sense" for both the actors and the viewing audience.

"Our release was bought by MGM and they took us over. It was pretty, pretty horrible so they sent us back to have the films made on Hal Roach's lot. Of course they [MGM] didn't want us running around the lot so we were only there for a little bit. We came out to MGM for publicity purposes and things but then we went right back to Hal Roach.

"What happened at that time was Hal Roach decided to make feature length pictures instead of two reel comedies. He sold Our Gang to MGM and soon found out he wasn't the greatest money maker in features that was known to man! Roach decided to make kid comedies again but there was only one problem. MGM didn't mind his making the kid comedies but they wouldn't give him back the Our Gang name!

"MGM kept the title 'Our Gang' and Hal Roach thought up the new name, 'Little Rascals.' I don't think they held after awhile; I think the silents were better. If you've watched the silents, the movies themselves were better, more *natural*. While we were shooting, our director, Bob McGowan would say, 'Jean, go over and take the doll away from Mary Ann' and I'd go over and take the doll away. Then he'd say, 'Mary Ann, you go over and run after Jean and get the doll back' and then 'Joe, you come over and stop the two girls arguing.'

Another *Our Gang* alumni: pretty little Mary Kornman, 1924.

"So we were doing the scene as we went along rather than rehearsing a scene. If you notice in the later talkies the children were *not* natural. When I was on the lot, we were *playing*. We were playing a game, like a barn dance and Bob McGowan was the caller.

"The children just didn't seem to be as natural when they were learning their lines. Take a film that is one of the silents and look at that, the way the kids act is so *natural*. Then look at one with dialogue. I don't know, it just seems to me that seeing them now, I think they were better in the beginning.

"Now of course, because of television, *everybody* thinks of the Gang as being the *talking* era. You see them and the kids are doing all kinds of things; they're singing, they're dancing. They are trying to be something the Gang wasn't. The Gang was just a bunch of kids *playing* and doing silly things!

"The most famous period of the Gang was, from about a year or two before I came into the Gang and maybe three years after I left. When I was with the Gang, we had out of town previews and the comedies were billed above the feature.

"Our Gang comedies came out on Saturdays and people flocked to see them! It was like when the first cartoons came out. Cartoons were the headliner. You'd have a Mickey Mouse or a Krazy Kat, then you would have a two reeler. It might be Laurel and Hardy which were still short comedies or some other short. Then the feature picture, a newsreel and then you had the trailors.

"That was what a film program was like then. Some theaters had five acts of vaudeville instead of the short subjects. Usually they had the newsreel with a live show and the trailors.

BLINDED BY THE LIGHT

"I was sitting out front watching the picture the way Mamma and I did between shows. Lots of times we'd run around out front and watch the movie for a little while if I wasn't doing homework or signing autographs, visiting children's hospitals and orphanages.

"I remember one day everything was blurry. It was just like that; bang! My eyes went and it was the klieg lights that blurred my eyesight. As you know, the carbon arcs are used outside in the street for openings or previews. Those great big huge lights and there are two poles of carbon.

"They are joined to create the light. This was *tremendously* bright but didn't last for a very long time. When I was a child, movies had moved inside a studio and so we used carbon arc lights which were called 'klieg lights.' Why everybody got klieg eyes [a common condition among early film actors which included burning, blurring, excessive tearing and in drastic cases, blindness, produced by over exposure to the kliegs] was because they were terribly, terribly powerful and secondly, after a few hours they would start to burn out.

"When they began to burn out, they were fascinating because as they died, they changed colors. They went through red then purple and then they'd go out. You just cannot imagine the *depth* of power of the color! Naturally if you're a child, what are you going to do? You'd have to *kill* them to make them not look!

Mary Ann Jackson and Jackie Cooper, March 1930 *Our Gang.*

"Even the adults looked but like I say, a lot of actors went blind because of the power of the light. They were *far* too powerful to use in a confined area. They would have so many [lights] on us. My goodness, they'd be up on the catwalks with these big arcs coming down on us. They'd have them on the floor around us and on the poles. Because so many people went blind, eventually they passed a law so that klieg lights couldn't be used indoors anymore."

Vaudeville

Jean Darling temporarily was "pulled" by her mother out of the Gang and thrust into the last golden days of vaudeville. Her description of those experiences are highly entertaining and very funny.

"I had a five year contract with Our Gang and stayed with them a little over four years. My mother wanted to put me in vaudeville which was dying on its feet! So she asked for a release even though I hadn't grown out of the Gang yet.

"But Mamma wanted me to go to vaudeville where *she* thought the money was. So before it *completely* collapsed, I was booked to headline a single act. I had been in vaudeville lots of times with the Gang. We went out every six months or so for a short tour and it was okay because we had a little routine of skits we did on stage. But then I was by *myself*, it was horrible!

"I had a tryout date in Elizabeth, New Jersey, and was taken to the theatre by [prizefighter/actor] Maxie Rosenbloom in his limousine. He had a big box of American Beauty roses. At that time, American Beauty roses had stems about thirty-six inches long with a teeny weenie little rose on top. I don't know why they were so fashionable or lovely with such tiny buds on top of such *huge* long stems!

"Maxie said he would give them to me over the footlights. When I came on stage, I couldn't make a sound! I was *frozen*. I looked at the audience and they looked at me and the orchestra played ... finally they pulled the curtain on me and my mother yanked me off stage.

"Well, Maxie just *left* us there and we had to take the milk train back to New York and walk home. He just didn't bother to come back because I was a flop. He just drove off. We were living at the Empire Hotel which was Sixty Third and Broadway. It was near the Professional Children's School where I went to school whenever I was in New York.

"The next morning Jack Dempsey called us up and he heard what Maxie Rosenbloom had done. He said he wanted to give him another cauliflower ear for the way he had treated us! Jack used to come out to the Roach Studio quite often and he liked me. He always brought me something.

"Anyway, he asked us to come over and meet him at a restaurant. He had a friend of his there who had a chain of thirty silent film theaters. Thirty tiny little theaters in New Jersey. Some of them only had one or two feet in front of the screen and an organ only for music. They took the film out of the projector and I did my act in the spotlight *from* the projector!

"I couldn't move much because I'd get out of the spot. The stages were so narrow; barely the width of my feet! If you try singing and dancing while worrying if you're going to fall off the stupid stage, you're going to quickly learn your job! Those thirty nights did the trick and for the next couple of years, I headlined a single act in vaudeville.

"My billing was 'Jean Darling in Person in an Act of Song, Dance and Patter.' I used to tell marvelous jokes like, 'The other day we were out on a farm making a movie and Wheezer saw a cow for the first time in his life. He asked what those funny things on the top of the cow's head were and Mr. McGowen said, "they're horns" and just then, the cow went "moooo" and Wheezer asked, "*Which* horn did the cow blow?" That was one of my prize jokes! This is the only one I remember fortunately!

"It is very difficult for performers today. On television you cannot perfect your performance. You cannot work things out. When you travel around playing different cities, the audiences in each city are *different.* You can have a joke that will absolutely *floor* people in one place and go on to the next city and the audience sits on their hands. They just look at you. So you try out jokes and songs until you finally have an act that works well *everywhere.*"

Yet another silent film child star, Frank "Junior" Coghlan, remembers his situation quite differently. Specifically, having a non-traditional stage mother who shied away from the limelight for both her and her son.

"I attribute much of my success to my lovely mother who kept me a 'nice' boy and never bothered the directors as so many of the other 'movie mothers' did while trying to promote their 'little darlings.' My mother always stayed in the background and made me say, 'Yes sir,' and 'No sir,' and always made me address the directors as "Mr." and not by their first names as so many other kid actors did, thinking it was 'cute.'

Our Gang as portrayed to European audiences. Joe Cobb, Mary Ann Jackson, Bobby "Wheezer" Hutchins, Jean Darling, Allen "Farina" Hoskins, Harry Spear and Pete the Dog.

"I think after one role with these directors they welcomed me back due to the respectful treatment they received from me and my mother. I certainly [do] blame my father for living beyond our means and causing us to lose the apartment house we had purchased during the 'depression.' In no way do I blame my lovely mother. She was truly an angel and put up with more than any lady was expected to endure from a drunken husband."

NO REASON FOR BITTERNESS

"A lot of the people you talk to will have a certain amount of bitterness in their memories, don't they? Which I think is so silly. I mean you look at their faces and some of them I could name look like the back end of a horse going west! They look so bitter that they hardly look like *faces* anymore. They look like they need to be sent out to be ironed or something.

"I think this is so silly. You haven't seen pictures of me now but I don't look bitter. I don't look mean and I don't look ugly! Some of it was fun and some of it wasn't. My mother was a 'stage mother' and she carried a switch in her purse. I felt that quite frequently in places where it didn't show.

"She was a very difficult mother. If you want to talk about mental cruelty, I had a great *deal* of mental cruelty. She was *always* going to kill herself if I wasn't a good girl and all this kind of nonsense.

"When I was seventeen years old I went to the window one day, opened it and said I was going to the library to change my books. It was a Sunday in New York City. She said she was going to jump if I left!

"I said, 'Okay, jump! But if you don't jump, I'll bring you ice cream when I come home.' So I brought her ice cream and that was the end of that.

"I remember once when I was very small, I was about eight years old. I went downstairs in the hotel to get a newspaper and when I came up, Mamma was lying in the bath tub full of water looking up at me with her big blue eyes! She was drowning herself!

"Now this can be rather unsettling! But I'm not bitter. I think it's funny. What would I have done? You know, most people when they grow up, remember going to maybe a pajama party or going to the prom *or* somebody knocking you off your bicycle.

"Well I have a whole *lot* of things I can remember. It's wonderful! Besides, I was never a child so I can be one *now!* I mean what would I have done? I would have just been a child and nothing would have happened to me. I decided I would have done what I was doing anyway, so then I didn't have to be mad at that anymore so I have nothing to be mad at.

"I was so young in the Gang, you really couldn't have a lot of fun, not when you're so little. There was a great deal of difference in ages. But I started having fun with people when I got to my flirtatious stage at six and *all* the boys were trying to have their box lunches with me. Then that was fine! I would sit there and let them bring me gifts and then I would choose which gift I liked best!

"Whether it was pebbles or a mirror, the quicksilver or whatever it was, if I liked the gift that was brought then I would have lunch with them! One brought me snake rattles, I had lunch with him too! I *loved* box lunches, I don't know why. They had hard boiled eggs and cheese sandwiches. We all liked them so much that when we weren't on location, they would trundle them out to the back lot from the commissary."

THE CHILD CELEBRITY

"When the studio sent me to Los Angeles to buy a dress, *everyone* in the department store would come running with awe and excitement! They'd stand me up on the counter and say, 'Ahhh, look at the lace on her petticoat, oh isn't that *lovely*, isn't that wonderful!' You're *never* going to recapture the celebrity you had as a child.

"You become a grown up and you will *never* attain this wonderful celebrity again. Some child stars are in Hollywood after they grow up waiting for a bus marked 'stardom' that's *never* going to come.

"And naturally, they are going to be bitter, aren't they? Then they start blaming the loss of childhood for everything that disappoints them. There's only one person who screws up my life and that's *me!* It's not my mother's fault, she's dead! If I open my mouth and say something I shouldn't, if I goof and I forget something, *I forgot it!* Once you get to the point in life where you realize that *you* are the master of your own ship, you can sink or swim.

"Once the BBC was doing a series about the Gang. They interviewed Jackie Cooper. Now Jackie Cooper has done *wonderful* things as an adult. He's directed, been in big movies, had his own programs. If he had come into the business when he was twenty-one years old he would have been very proud of himself.

"He wrote a letter to the *Radio Times* in London saying that all the kids who were in movies were *ruined,* destroyed. They were drug addicts, prostitutes or had to go to shrinks or something. Their lives were ruined and they were all divorced, and he went on and on.

"Well *I* wrote a letter to the *Radio Times* in London and said I'd only been married once, I only had one child, I never went to a shrink and I never even slept with John F. Kennedy! He made this blanket statement that this entire group of people were destroyed, were dysfunctional. *I AM NOT!* Don't sound dysfunctional, do I? It's easier to blame your failure on something else rather than *yourself.*

"I've always felt that you go through life with your hand open and you don't get hit nearly as often as when you have a chip on your shoulder. I hold my son very tightly with an opened hand. I don't write and I don't phone him unless I have to. That way you can stay friends much longer than if you try to cling.

"He's his own man and when I fall off the porch, he'll be sad I'm gone but he will be free. For me, today is today. I might not have a tomorrow. You see, I almost died when I was about twenty. I think it's the best thing that ever happened to me.

"I was on the critical list for three months. I had infectious hepatitis and had complete liver failure. They didn't think I'd live. When I went into the hospital everything seemed black and white. And when I came out, the world was *beautiful,* filled with color. When it's night you notice each little mica flash in the pavement is different from the other little mica flash. You notice *everything!* I still notice everything. Everybody should die for awhile; it would straighten them out!

LOSS OF FILMS AND ENTER SOUND

Jean Darling, like so many other silent film era stars, remembers the tragic loss of so many early films, including her own. She also remembers the transition from silent to sound and some pretty special people she met along the way.

"I'll tell you about the destruction of silent film which is also not mentioned in any book that I know of. There was a little stone or brick house on the lot where many films were stored. I had my picture taken in front of this little storage house. I imagine it was about eighteen feet by twelve feet. In it were 'Our Gang' films, Harold Lloyd films, Charlie Chase, Laurel & Hardy, Harry Langdon, everything. One day the films combusted.

"And the crossover into talkies was just idiocy on the part of the producers! Instead of thinking a star could go on and have some voice coaching, they would immediately drop anybody on the first squawk! They went to the stage and brought over stage actors because they would have good voices."

ON THE MGM LOT

"[Actor] Herbert Marshall was very nice to me because I heard he had a wooden leg. At the time, I was past the Gang and was going to the St. Augustinian Church across the street from MGM. I heard he had a wooden leg so I went over to the set of *The Painted Veil* with Greta Garbo. I was allowed to run around loose because Our Gang had been with MGM.

"I saw Mr. Marshall sitting in his director's chair, reading the script. I came over and leaned on the arm of his chair and sort of idly as though it was an accident, put my hand on his knee and tapped it. Then I went over on the other side and did the same thing and he said, 'It's the right one! Why didn't you *ask* which one?' I answered, 'I didn't want to be rude!'

"I liked Patsy Kelly and ZaSu Pitts. I liked Patsy but ZaSu was lovely. William Powell was always very nice to me. I would go around fantasizing people as daddies. Clark Gable found me under a desk once, reading Fu Manchu. Gable pulled me out. He got very upset that I was reading Fu Manchu because I was maybe seven. When he found me again, he had the *Blue Fairy Tale Book* in his pocket. He took me in the office next door, took me in his lap and read fairy tales! It was nice because he wanted a child and I wanted a daddy and so for awhile it was nice.

"Things are better when you're broke. It's more fun when you're climbing the ladder than when you get to the top. That's what Marie Dressler said to me when she won an Oscar, I think, for *Min and Bill* [MGM 1930]. She said, 'Well what do I do now?' She was the one who advised me that when you get to the top of the ladder to go find *another* ladder to climb.

Laurel and Hardy talk to *Our Gang* members. (L–R): Harry Spear, Mary Ann Jackson, Farina, Pete the dog, Joe Cobb and Jean Darling, circa 1927.

"We were going down Hollywood Boulevard and in Santa Claus' sleigh, Wampas Baby Stars in brief little skating costumes were draped around the sleigh. 'What will they do when they are not pretty anymore?' Marie Dressler added. 'I was never pretty so I had to *learn* my trade.'

LIFE IN IRELAND TODAY

Jean Darling has lived in Ireland since 1974. When I ask her when she moved there, she answered briskly, "We never moved here, we just stopped!"

"My husband Kajar the Magician was booked into the Olympia Theatre here in Dublin. And as you could store props at CIE, which was the transportation terminal for buses and trains, for two pounds a month, we moved our base here but we didn't come here to live until 1974.

"After my son and I were in Dublin for awhile, a cat moved in. She looked like she'd been pulled through an exhaust pipe backwards! We rented a garden flat and [we] couldn't have a cat. Then she got in trouble and I thought, 'I am *not* going to throw this little unwed mother out!'

"Finally when we wanted to move, we tried and tried but we couldn't find any place to go so we had to buy a house for the cat!

"There weren't any serious problems here at that time. Not until 1969, then problems flared up again in the North which are based on events that began eight hundred years ago! How can you worry about things that happened eight hundred years ago? You've got to get on with life."

Jean Darling knows celebrity as an adult as well. From years on Broadway, her best known role was as Carrie Pipperidge in the original Broadway production of *Carousel*. Plus she has written dozens of short mystery stories for Ellery Queen, Hitchcock and Mike Shayne, as well as numerous horror-fantasy tales. She is also a journalist and delights in writing plays for radio (RTE and SABC).

A writer of hundreds of children's stories, she is a storyteller of great renown. Listening to her wonderfully funny and animated speech, it is impossible to imagine her young audiences as less than captivated. And the beautiful and funny little blonde girl from Our Gang seems very happy in her maturity.

"I'm Aunty Poppy here because I was born in California and the poppy is the California flower. Now I have two cats and a dog. Why two cats? I have two windows in the front of the house and I didn't want to be lopsided, so I have a cushion on the table in each window so that the cats can look out. So there!"

Indeed, Jean Darling has led a very interesting life. And she still does so, with or without the Gang!

FILMOGRAPHY

Seeing the World—1927. Pathé. *Director:* Robert F. McGowan. *Producer:* Hal Roach. *Cast:* Joe Cobb, Allen "Farina" Hoskins, Jackie Condon, Johnny Downs, Peggy Eames, Scooter Lowry, Jay R. Smith, Jean Darling, Stan Laurel. **Ten Years Old**—1927. Pathé. *Director:* Anthony Mack. *Producer:* Hal Roach. *Cast:* Joe Cobb, Bobby

Young, Jean Darling, Allen "Farina" Hoskins, Jackie Condon, Jannie Hoskins, Mildred Kornman, Jay R. Smith, Johnny Aber, Scooter Lowry, Bret Black, Peggy Eames.

Bring Home the Turkey—1927. Pathé. *Director:* Robert F. McGowan, Anthony Mack. *Producer:* Hal Roach. *Cast:* Joe Cobb, Allen "Farina" Hoskins, Jean Darling, Johnny Downs, Scooter Lowry, Jannie "Mango" Hoskins, Jackie Condon, Peggy Eames, Jay R. Smith, Mildred Kornman, Noah Young.

Tired Business Man—1927. Pathé. *Directors:* Anthony Mack, Charles Oelze. *Producer:* Hal Roach. *Cast:* Jackie Condon, Jean Darling, Jannie Hoskins, Allen "Farina" Hoskins, Bobby Young, Joe Cobb, Jay R. Smith, Peggy Eames, Johnny Aber, Bobby Mallon, Scooter Lowry, Billy Butts.

Baby Brother—1927. Pathé. *Directors:* Anthony Mack, Charles Oelze. *Producer:* Hal Roach. *Cast:* Jackie Condon, Jean Darling, Joe Cobb, Allen "Farina" Hoskins, Scooter Lowry, Bobby Young, Jay R. Smith, Jannie Hoskins, Mildred Kornman, Bobby "Wheezer" Hutchins, Donnie Smith.

Chicken Feed—1927. Pathé. *Directors:* A. Mack, Charles Oelze. *Producer:* Hal Roach. *Cast:* Johnny Downs, Jean Darling, Jay R. Smith, Scooter Lowry, Harry Spear, Bobby "Wheezer" Hutchins, Bobby Mallon, Bobby Young, Joe Cobb, Jackie Condon.

Olympic Games—1927. Pathé. *Director:* Anthony Mack. *Producer:* Hal Roach. *Cast:* Allen "Farina" Hoskins, Jean Darling, Joe Cobb, Jay R. Smith, Jackie Condon, Bobby "Wheezer" Hutchins, Mildred Kornman, Peggy Ahearn, Harry Spear, Jannie Hoskins, Scooter Lowry, Johnny Aber, Joseph Metzger, Pete the Dog.

Yale vs. Harvard—1927. MGM. *Director:* Robert F. McGowan. *Producer:* Hal Roach. *Cast:* Allen "Farina" Hoskins, Harry Spear, Jean Darling, Jackie Condon, Joe Cobb, Jay R. Smith, Jannie Hoskins, Pete the Dog.

The Old Wallop—1927. MGM. *Director:* Robert F. McGowan. *Producer:* Robert F. McGowan. *Cast:* Joe Cobb, Jean Darling, Harry Spear, Jay. R. Smith, Bobby "Wheezer" Hutchins, Allen "Farina" Hoskins, Jackie Condon.

Heebee Jeebees—1927. MGM. *Director:* Anthony Mack. *Producer:* Robert F. McGowan. *Cast:* Bobby "Wheezer" Hutchins, Jackie Condon, Harry Spear, Joe Cobb, Jean Darling, Jay R. Smith, Allen "Farina" Hoskins, Pete the Dog.

Dog Heaven—1927. MGM. *Director:* Anthony Mack. *Producer:* Robert F. McGowan. *Cast:* Bobby "Wheezer" Hutchins, Jean Darling, Joe Cobb, Jackie Condon, Jay R. Smith, Mildred Kornman, Allen "Farina" Hoskins, Pete the Dog.

Spook Spoofing—1928. MGM. *Director:* Robert F. McGowan. *Producer:* Robert F. McGowan. *Cast:* Johnny Aber, Jean Darling, Bobby "Wheezer" Hutchins, Joe Cobb, Jay R. Smith, Mildred

Kornman, Harry Spear, Allen "Farina" Hoskins, Jackie Condon, Pete the Dog.

Rainy Days—1928. MGM. *Director:* Anthony Mack. *Producer:* Robert F. McGowan. *Cast:* Jay R. Smith, Jean Darling, Bobby "Wheezer" Hutchins, Jackie Condon, Joe Cobb, Allen "Farina" Hoskins, Harry Spear, Mildred Kornman, Pete the Dog.

Edison, Marconi & Co.—1928. MGM. *Director:* Anthony Mack. *Producer:* Hal Roach. *Cast:* Jean Darling, Bobby "Wheezer" Hutchins, Jackie Condon, Jay R. Smith, Harry Spear, Allen "Farina" Hoskins, Mildred Kornman, Joe Cobb, Pete the Dog.

Barnum & Ringling, Inc.—1928. MGM. *Director:* Robert F. McGowan. *Producer:* Robert F. McGowan. *Cast:* Allen "Farina" Hoskins, Jean Darling, Joe Cobb, Jay R. Smith, Bobby "Wheezer" Hutchins, Mildred Kornman, Jackie Condon, Harry Spear, Johnny Aber, Oliver Hardy, Edna Marion, Eugene Pallette, Pete the Dog.

Fair and Muddy—1928. MGM. *Director:* Charley Oelze. *Producer:* Hal Roach. *Cast:* Jackie Condon, Jay R. Smith, Jean Darling, Joe Cobb, Bobby "Wheezer" Hutchins, Mildred Kornman, Harry Spear, Allen "Farina" Hoskins, Pete the Dog.

Crazy House—1928. MGM. *Director:* Robert F. McGowan. *Producer:* Robert F. McGowan. *Cast:* Mary Ann Jackson, Bobby "Wheezer" Hutchins, Harry Spear, Jean Darling, Joe Cobb, Jackie Condon, Jay R. Smith, Allen 'Farina' Hoskins, Pete the Dog.

Growing Pains—1928. MGM. *Director:* Anthony Mack. *Producer:* Robert F. McGowan. *Cast:* Allen "Farina" Hoskins, Jean Darling, Joe Cobb, Jackie Condon, Jay R. Smith, Mary Ann Jackson, Harry Spear, Bobby "Wheezer" Hutchins, Pete the Dog.

Old Gray Hoss—1928. MGM. *Director:* Anthony Mack. *Producer:* Robert F. McGowan. *Cast:* Harry Spear, Allen "Farina" Hoskins, Bobby "Wheezer" Hutchins, Mary Ann Jackson, Jean Darling, Joe Cobb, Pete the Dog.

School Begins—1928. MGM. *Director:* Anthony Mack. *Producer:* Robert F. McGowan. *Cast:* Harry Spear, Joe Cobb, Bobby "Wheezer" Hutchins, Allen "Farina" Hoskins, Jean Darling, Mary Ann Jackson, Pete the Dog.

The Spanking Age—1928. MGM. *Director:* Robert F. McGowan. *Producer:* Hal Roach. *Cast:* Joe Cobb, Jean Darling, Allen "Farina" Hoskins, Harry Spear, Mary Ann Jackson, Bobby "Wheezer" Hutchins, Pete the Dog.

Playin' Hookey—1928. Pathé. *Director:* Anthony Mack. *Producer:* Hal Roach. *Cast:* Joe Cobb, Harry Spear, Jean Darling, Jannie Hoskins, Bobby "Wheezer" Hutchins, Jackie Condon, Jay R. Smith, Allen "Farina" Hoskins, Pete the Dog.

The Smile Wins—1928. Pathé. *Director:* Robert F. McGowan. *Producer:* Hal Roach. *Cast:* Jean Darling, Joe Cobb, Harry Spear, Bobby "Wheezer" Hutchins, Jackie Condon, Jannie Hoskins, Jay R.

Smith, Allen "Farina" Hoskins, Pete the Dog.

Noisy Noises—1929. MGM. *Director:* Robert F. McGowan. *Producer:* Robert F. McGowan. *Cast:* Mary Ann Jackson, Harry Spear, Joe Cobb, Bret Black, Jean Darling, Gordon Thorpe, Allen "Farina" Hoskins, Bobby "Wheezer" Hut-chins, Jay R. Smith, Pete the Dog.

The Holy Terror—1929. MGM. *Director:* Anthony Mack. *Producer:* Robert F. McGowan. *Cast:* Harry Spear, Jean Darling, Allen "Farina" Hoskins, Mary Ann Jackson, Joe Cobb, Bobby "Wheezer" Hutchins, Pete the Dog.

Wiggle Your Ears—1929. MGM. *Director:* Robert F. McGowan. *Producer:* Robert F. McGowan. *Cast:* Jean Darling, Harry Spear, Allen "Farina" Hoskins, Joe Cobb, Mary Ann Jackson, Bobby "Wheezer" Hutchins, Pete the Dog.

Fast Freight—1929. MGM. *Director:* Anthony Mack. *Producer:* Robert F. McGowan. *Cast:* Jean Darling, Bobby "Wheezer" Hutchins, Mary Ann Jackson, Harry Spear, Joe Cobb, Allen "Farina" Hoskins, Pete the Dog.

Little Mother—1929. MGM. *Director:* Robert F. McGowan. *Producer:* Robert F. McGowan. *Cast:* Mary Ann Jackson, Joe Cobb, Bobby "Wheezer" Hutchins, Jean Darling, Harry Spear, Donnie Smith, Allen "Farina" Hoskins, Pete the Dog.

Cat, Dog & Co.—1929. MGM. *Director:* Anthony Mack. *Producer:* Robert F. McGowan. *Cast:* Joe Cobb, Mary Ann Jackson, Harry Spear, Jean Darling, Allen "Farina" Hoskins, Donnie Smith,

Bobby "Wheezer" Hutchins, Hedda Hopper, Pete the Dog.

Saturday's Lesson—1929. MGM. *Director:* Robert F. McGowan. *Producer:* Robert F. McGowan. *Cast:* Mary Ann Jackson, Jean Darling, Bobby "Wheezer" Hutchins, Harry Spear, Allen "Farina" Hoskins, Joe Cobb, Pete the Dog.

Small Talk—1929. MGM. *Director:* Robert F. McGowan. *Producer:* Robert F. McGowan. *Cast:* Harry Spear, Jean Darling, Joe Cobb, Allen "Farina" Hoskins, Mary Ann Jackson, Bobby "Wheezer" Hutchins, Pete the Dog.

Railroadin'—1929. MGM. *Director:* Robert F. McGowan. *Producer:* Robert F. McGowan. *Cast:* Joe Cobb, Jean Darling, Harry Spear, Bobby "Wheezer" Hutchins, Mary Ann Jackson, Allen "Farina" Hoskins, Norman "Chubby" Chaney, Pete the Dog.

Boxing Gloves—1929. MGM. *Director:* Anthony Mack. *Producer:* Hal Roach. *Cast:* Allen "Farina" Hoskins, Harry Spear, Jean Darling, Bobby "Wheezer" Hutchins, Joe Cobb, Mary Ann Jackson, Jackie Cooper, Donnie Smith, Johnny Aber, Billy Schuler, Bobby Mallon, Norman "Chubby" Chaney, Pete the Dog.

Lazy Days—1929. MGM. *Director:* Robert F. McGowan. *Producer:* Robert F. McGowan. *Cast:* Mary Ann Jackson, Jean Darling, Joe Cobb, Norman "Chubby" Chaney, Bobbie Burns, Harry Spear, Allen "Farina" Hoskins, Jannie Hoskins, Bobby "Wheezer" Hutchins, Pete the Dog.

Bouncing Babies—1929. MGM. *Director:* Robert F. McGowan. *Producer:* Robert F. McGowan.

Cast: Mary Ann Jackson, Allen "Farina" Hoskins, Jean Darling, Jackie Cooper, Bobby Mallon, Harry Spear, Joe Cobb, Tommy Atkins, Bobby "Wheezer" Hutchins, Norman "Chubby" Chaney, Pete the Dog.

Only Yesterday—1933. Universal Pictures. *Director:* John M. Stahl. *Producer:* Carl Laemmle, Jr. *Writing:* Frederick Lewis Allen, William Hurlbut, George O'Neil, Arthur Richman, Stefan Zweig. *Cast:* Margaret Sullavan, John Boles, Billie Burke, Reginald Denny, Jimmy Butler, Edna May Oliver, Benita Hume, George Meeker, June Clyde, Marie Prevost, Oscar Apfel, Jane Darwell, Tom Conlon, Berton Churchill, Onslow Stevens, Walter Catlett, Noel Frances, Franklin Pangborn, Barry Norton, Arthur Hoyt, Natalie Moorhead, Joyce Compton, Betty Blythe, Grady Sutton, Ruth Clifford, Dorothy Christy, Julia Faye, Bramwell Fletcher, Crauford Kent, Vivien Oakland, Astrid Allwyn, King Baggot, Ben Bard, Frank Beal, Louise Beavers, Robert Bolder, Sidney Bracey, Edmund Breese, Marion Byron, Julie Carter, Lita Chevret, Harvey Clark, Marion Clayton, Sammy Cohen, Herbert Corthell, Lynn Cowan, Ida Darling, Jean Darling, William B. Davidson, James Donlan, Mary Doran, Norma Drew, Robert Ellis, Cissy Fitzgerald, James Flavin, Charles K. French, Hans Fuerberg, Huntley Gordon, Dorothy Granger, George Hackathorne, Creighton Hale, Jeanne Hart, Otto Hoffman, Virginia Howell, George Irving, Eleanor Jackson, Eddie Kane, Natalie Kingston, Florence Lake, Caryl Lincoln, Herta Lynd, Sheila Manners, Mabel Marden, Deacon McDaniels, Matt McHugh, Ferdinand Munier, Edgar Norton, Tom O'Brien, Lucille Powers, Craig Reynolds, Jack Richardson, Bert Roach, Jason Robards Sr., Churchill Ross, Gay Seabrook, Jeanne Sorel, Warren Stokes, Richard Tucker, Maidel Turner, Bruce Warren, Mildred Washington, Leon Waycroft, Leo White, Lloyd Whitlock, Lyman Williams, Dick Winslow.

Jane Eyre—1934. Monogram Pictures. *Director:* Christy Cabanne. *Producer:* Bert Verschleiser. *Music:* Abe Meyer. *Cinematography:* Robert H. Planck. *Writing:* Charlotte Brontë (novel), Adele Commandini. *Cast:* Virginia Bruce, Colin Clive, Beryl Mercer, David Torrence, Aileen Pringle, Edith Fellows, John Rogers, Jean Darling, Lionel Belmore, Jameson Thomas, Ethel Griffies, Claire Du Brey, William Burress, Joan Standing, Richard Quine, Gretta Gould, Anne Howard, Olaf Hytten, Gail Kaye, Edith Kingston, Desmond Roberts, Clarissa Selwynne, Hylda Tyson, William Wagner.

Babes in Toyland—1934. Hal Roach Studios/MGM. *Directors:* Gus Meins, Charles Rogers. *Producers:* Hal Roach. (Also known as **Laurel and Hardy in Toyland, March of the Wooden Soldiers, Revenge Is Sweet and Wooden Soldiers.**) *Writing:* Frank Butler, Nick Grinde, Victor Herbert (operetta), Glen MacDonough (operetta). *Music:* Victor Herbert. Cinematography Francis Corby, Art

Lloyd. *Cast:* Stan Laurel, Oliver Hardy, Virginia Karns, Charlotte Henry, Felix Knight, Florence Roberts, Henry Brandon, Frank Austin, Eddie Baker, Billie Bletcher, Tommy Bupp, William Burress, Alice Dahl, Jean Darling, Johnny Downs, John George, Sumner Getchell, Pete Gordon, Dickie Jones, Gus Leonard, Alice Moore, Kewpie Morgan, Ferdinand Munier, Margaret Nearing, Charles Rogers, Carl Russell, Marie Wilson.

Douglas Fairbanks, Jr.

One cannot speak about the early years of Hollywood without mentioning the big three: Douglas Fairbanks, Sr., Charlie Chaplin and Mary Pickford. Along with director D. W. Griffith, they were responsible for forming United Artists Studio, and their film legacies continue to survive the constraints of time. But could a son or daughter of one of these film giants have the same success in the shadow of such a cinema role? Well one did and has maintained a career which has literally spanned decades.

Douglas Fairbanks, Jr., was anxious to talk about those early years in Hollywood. We talked about his father, Miss Pickford, Chaplin, Joan Crawford and much more. One legend following another, Mr. Fairbanks recalled that glorious past and the center of Hollywood royalty, Pickfair.

"I didn't get up there very much because I was living with my mother at the time. When my father was away, my cousins and I would go up and have a swim in the pool. I have very pleasant memories of it. Sometimes my father and I would play jokes on guests visiting out of town."

Pickfair was the social equinox at that time. Whether it be presidents, politicians or movie stars, the estate of Doug Sr. and Mary was the place to be invited. Not until Valentino's Falcon's Lair would a Hollywood residence hold so many memories or represent the magic of a Hollywood which exists no longer.

"I was devoted to her [Mary Pickford], she was terribly sweet to me. The moment I first met her as a very young boy, I thought, 'She is so small!' I thought she was a little girl of my age group who had come to play with me. When I found out she was a grown woman I was so surprised!

"There weren't wild parties [at Pickfair] of any kind, they were pretty formal as a matter of fact. They were pretty respectable parties."

Fairbanks Jr. didn't exactly receive a huge cheer from his dad when he too wanted to enter films. "He preferred that I finish school and go to the university and then decide. He didn't want me to start as young as I did and he was right. Both my parents were divorced at the time and I was being brought up by my mother.

"My mother thought it was a good idea. It meant more money and so forth. When I was out of a [film] job I was given

Douglas Fairbanks, Jr., in 1924 (photograph by Richee).

the job of writing subtitles for silent films and that came in very handy. I wrote some of the subtitles for one of my father's films, *The Gaucho* [1927], and rewrote others. I don't even remember the ones I did write but I wrote quite a number."

GRETA, LORETTA AND JOAN

Like his father, Doug Jr. had the opportunity to meet and work with some of the biggest names in the business. He had worked with Garbo in *A Woman of Affairs* (1928) which also co-starred John Gilbert and Lewis Stone.

"Well I've known her off stage as well, away from the daily work. I have always been very fond of her. She was an awfully nice woman and not a tragic [or] dramatic character that one thinks of her being. She was very normal, laughed a lot, loved to play jokes and lovely to work with. Everybody liked her.

"Loretta [Young] and I made about seven or eight pictures together. She was lovely to work with, absolutely lovely. We were such good friends. I used to take her sister [Sally Blane] out to the movies [on] weekends and parties. I didn't go out with her as a big romance but we did go out. I was very close to the family. Her family and my four girl cousins were all friends of Loretta's. Her real name was Gretchen, we all called her Gretch."

Douglas Fairbanks, Jr., and "ambitious" wife Joan Crawford.

Joan Crawford would end up being Mrs. Fairbanks, Jr., and I was naturally curious as to whether Crawford was as ambitious or mean spirited as she's often portrayed.

"Yes, Miss Crawford was very ambitious. However, I cannot speak of her as being 'mean spirited.' I saw only the agreeable part of her. I have read and heard various stories but I don't recall having experienced that in our association. I don't say she *wasn't* like that but I never was a witness to it.

"She wrote me a fan letter after seeing the opening night of a play I was in called *Young Woodley* and invited me to have a cup of tea with her or something like that one night. [She] began writing me fan letters. She broke the ice and invited me."

CHAPLIN AND BARRYMORE

"I had known him [Chaplin] since I was about four or five years old. I have all sorts of charming memories. He was wonderful with children. Sometimes when older grown-ups were too bored to play with me, Charlie would ride on my wagon with me and play games and play with

Loretta Young, circa 1928 (photograph by Harold Dean Carsey).

me in the swimming pool. Then when I grew up we became good friends. I was a boy and he was a grown man but he was always wonderful with me.

"John Barrymore was one of my great theatrical heroes. I just thought he was marvelous and he had also been very good with me. I had a serious crush on his sister-in-law Helene Costello. He was married to Dolores Costello and I used to go out with Helene. I thought if I ever married her I would become the brother-in-law of Jack!

"Actually, they [the Barrymores] were bigger on stage than they were in the movies. They were the biggest stars we had on the stage, of anybody. Talent and God-given personality, all the Barrymores had, in that same unique way."

MAKING THE CROSSOVER

Fairbanks Jr.'s career in film, radio, stage and television ended up spanning decades. He credits in part his success in the early training he received.

"Those who succeeded best were those who had been trained for the theatre [and] had good voices. I had been on the stage first and had taken voice lessons and all sorts of training for the stage; movement, dance, voice placement."

One of his earliest, and fondest recollections was a stage production he had done with director Max Reinhardt.

Like father, like son: Doug Jr. and Doug Sr. in 1924.

The happy couple: Fairbanks Jr. and Crawford.

"That was an all star production of *A Midsummer Night's Dream*. [Reinhardt] was very easy to work with. He had a very delicate touch of directing and got the best out of people. Not with yelling and screaming but just gently talking to them."

Once sound films had replaced silents, many less fortunate actors found themselves out on the street and many silent films [were] deliberately destroyed for fear of competition. Not recognizing the silent film as a true art form, former stars and their films were now considered antiquated and at worst, grotesque.

Partly because the early sound was technically inadequate and actors now had to move or stay in place within the constraints of the microphones, one either made a successful crossover or not. At least with vocal training, the silent stars had a greater chance at achieving success in talkies.

"A lot of it was newspapers and just making a lot of publicity about it. But some of them were disappointing. I just remember that it happened and [there] was quite a hot discussion about it at the time. The *quality* of acting and directing became more sophisticated as time went on."

Did Mr. Fairbanks prefer sound pictures or silent? "That really depends on the stories. Some stories are best told in the least amount of speech and more action. Films were really made [then] as well as they could be made. I think on the stage is the most gratifying goal to

Douglas Fairbanks As THE BLACK PIRATE ~

Douglas Fairbanks, Sr.: dashing, athletic, a Hollywood legend. Circa 1926.

the person connecting with the audience, but in the end result, I like motion pictures.

"For silent films I worked mostly outside on location, mainly because of the natural light which gave the camera man better control. The [klieg] lights were very harsh and brought pain to the eyes, inspiring several lawsuits. In between scenes when not filming, we would wear dark glasses to shield our eyes.

(One of America's greatest actresses, Lillian Gish, summed up the urgency that early directors and camera crewmen placed upon the importance of natural sunlight while filming. In her autobiography *The Movies, Mr. Griffith, and Me* she stated: "As always, sunlight controlled the shooting schedule. Preparations began at five or six in the morning. The actors rose at five in order to ready at seven, when it was bright enough for filming. Important scenes were played in the hard noon sun. I remember that we used to beg to have our closeups taken just after dawn or before sunset, as the soft yellow glow was easier to work in and much more flattering. We continued to work—often without a break for lunch—until sundown.")

"On the other hand, talkies had to be filmed indoors in the beginning. In silent films there was no need to learn the text [although] the closer one came to the text, the more effective the scene was (however this seems obvious).

"Often foreigners who could barely speak any English whatsoever became universally popular, particularly in English speaking countries. Rudolph Valentino was an example whose popularity as a great lover was unmatched regardless *what* language he chose to speak.

"The *quality* of acting and directing became more sophisticated as time went on.

"I was with Warner Bros. and First National for awhile and then I had a limited deal with MGM for three or four pictures. Then I freelanced for a long time and then started my own company abroad in England."

With the mention of MGM, I was very curious as to how Mr. Fairbanks would remember L.B. Mayer, the studio's tyrannical head.

"I was terrified of him as most people were. He wasn't really nasty [to work with] but in a subtle way, very strong, and people were very frightened of him. He could be nice too but a lot of people were under contract and were really very terrified of him. He came to my house for dinner a couple of times.

"[We] were saved by Irving Thalberg who married Norma Shearer who was more of an intellectual and very easy and pleasant to get along with. I liked him very much. [Shearer] was very pleasant indeed. Not much to say about her. She's very respectable, very quiet, very dignified. Not very jolly you know, she's not a very gay person, I mean gay in the old sense of the word meaning very dignified, quiet and concentrating on her work."

I thanked Mr. Fairbanks for the interview and while bringing it to a close, asked him how he'd like to be remembered. After all, he was and is a legend in every sense.

"You know what they say about legends ... legend is a story very often told but not necessarily true," he replied modestly.

FILMOGRAPHY

Stephen Steps Out—1923. Famous Players/Lasky. *Director:* Joseph Henabery. *Released by* Paramount. *Cast:* Theodore Roberts, Douglas Fairbanks, Jr., Noah Beery, Harry Myers, Fannie Midgley.

The Air Mail—1924. Famous Players/Lasky. *Director:* Irvin Willat. *Cast:* Warner Baxter, Billie Dove, Douglas Fairbanks, Jr., Mary Brian.

The American Venus—1925. Famous Players/Lasky. *Director:* Frank Tuttle. *Cast:* Esther Ralston, Lawrence Gray, Ford Sterling, Fay Lamphier, Louise Brooks, Edna May Oliver, Kenneth MacKenna, William B. Mack, George DeCarlton, W.T. Benda, Ernest Torrence, Douglas Fairbanks, Jr.

Wild Horse Mesa—1925. Famous Players/Lasky. *Director:* George B. Seitz. *Cast:* Jack Holt, Noah Beery, Billie Dove, Douglas Fairbanks, Jr.

Stella Dallas—1925. Samuel Goldwyn, Inc. *Director:* Henry King. *Cast:* Ronald Colman, Belle Bennett, Alice Joyce, Jean Hersholt, Lois Moran, Douglas Fairbanks, Jr.

Padlocked—1926. Famous Players/Lasky. *Director:* Allan Dwan. *Cast:* Lois Moran, Noah Beery, Louise Dresser, Helen Jerome Eddy, Douglas Fairbanks, Jr.

Broken Hearts of Hollywood—1926. Warner Bros. *Directors:* Lloyd Bacon. *Cast:* Patsy Ruth Miller, Louise Dresser, Douglas Fairbanks, Jr., Jerry Miley, Barbara Worth.

Man Bait—1926. Metropolitan Pictures. *Director:* Donald Crisp. *Cast:* Marie Prevost, Kenneth Thomson, Douglas Fairbanks, Jr., Louis Natheaux, Sally Rand.

Women Love Diamonds—1927. MGM *Director:* Edmund Goulding. *Cast:* Pauline Starke, Owen Moore, Lionel Barrymore, Cissy Fitzgerald, Gwen Lee, Douglas Fairbanks, Jr.

Is Zat So?—1927. Fox Film. *Director:* Alfred E. Green. *Cast:* George O'Brien, Edmund Lowe, Kathryn Perry, C. Chadwick, Doris Lloyd, Dione Ellis, Douglas Fairbanks, Jr.

A Texas Steer—1927. Sam E. Rork Prod. Released through First National. *Director:* Richard Wallace. *Cast:* Will Rogers, Louise Fazenda, Sam Hardy, Ann Rork, Douglas Fairbanks, Jr.

Dead Man's Curve—1928. FBO Pictures. *Director:* Richard Rosson. *Cast:* Douglas Fairbanks, Jr., Sally Blane, Charles Byer, Arthur Metcalf, Joel McCrea.

Modern Mothers—1928. Columbia. *Director:* Philip Rosen. *Cast:* Helene Chadwick, Ethel Grey Terry, Barbara Kent, Douglas Fairbanks, Jr.

The Toilers—1928. Tiffany-Stahl Prod. *Director:* Reginald Barker. *Cast:* Douglas Fairbanks, Jr., Jobyna Ralston, Harvey Clark, Wade Boteler, Robert Ryan.

The Power of the Press—1928. Columbia. *Director:* Frank Capra. *Cast:* Douglas Fairbanks, Jr., Jobyna Ralston, Mildred Harris, Philo McCullough, Wheeler Oakman.

A Woman of Affairs—1928. MGM. *Director:* Clarence Brown. *Cast:* Greta Garbo, John Gilbert, Lewis Stone, John Mack Brown, Douglas Fairbanks, Jr.

The Barker—1928. First National. *Director:* George Fitzmaurice. *Cast:* Milton Sills, Dorothy Mackaill, Betty Compson, Douglas Fairbanks, Jr., George Cooper, John Erwin.

The Jazz Age—1929. FBO Pictures. *Director:* Lynn Shores. *Cast:* Douglas Fairbanks, Jr., Marceline Day, Henry B. Walthall, Myrtle Stedman, Joel McCrea.

Fast Life—1929. First National. *Director:* John Francis Dillon. *Cast:* Douglas Fairbanks, Jr., Loretta Young, William Holden, Chester Morris, Frank Sheridan.

Our Modern Maidens—1929. MGM *Director:* Jack Conway. *Cast:* Joan Crawford, Rod LaRocque, Douglas Fairbanks, Jr., Anita Page, Edward Nugent.

The Careless Age—1929. First National. *Director:* John Griffith Wray. *Cast:* Douglas Fairbanks, Jr., Carmel Myers, Holmes Herbert, Kenneth Thompson, Loretta Young, Ilka Chase.

The Forward Pass—1929. First National. *Director:* Eddie Cline. *Cast:* Douglas Fairbanks, Jr., Loretta Young, Guinn Williams, Marion Byron, Phyllis Crane.

The Show of Shows—1929. Warner Bros. *Director:* John G. Adolfi. *Cast:* Frank Fay, William Courtenay, H.B. Warner, Hobart Bosworth, John Barrymore, Douglas Fairbanks, Jr., Chester Conklin, Lois Wilson.

Party Girl—1930. Victory Pictures/Tiffany. *Director:* Victor Halpenn. *Cast:* Douglas Fairbanks, Jr., Jeanette Lott, Judith Barne, Marie Prevost.

Loose Ankles—1930. First National. *Director:* Ted Wilde. *Cast:* Douglas Fairbanks, Jr., Loretta Young, Louise Fazenda, Ethel Wales, Daphne Pollard, O. Harlan.

Dawn Patrol—1930. First National.

Director: Howard Hawks. *Cast:* Richard Barthelmess, Neil Hamilton, Douglas Fairbanks, Jr., William Janney, James Finlayson.

The Little Accident—1930. Universal. *Director:* William James Craft. *Cast:* Anita Page, Douglas Fairbanks, Jr., Sally Blane, ZaSu Pitts, Roscoe Karns, Slim Summerville.

Outward Bound—1930. Warner Bros. Released through First National. *Director:* Robert Milton. *Cast:* Leslie Howard, Douglas Fairbanks, Jr., Helen Chandler, Beryl Mercer, Alison Skipworth, Montagu Love, Dudley Digges, Lyonel Watts.

The Way of All Men—1930. First National. (Re-make of 1922 film, **The Sin Flood.**) *Director:* Frank Lloyd. *Cast:* Douglas Fairbanks, Jr., Dorothy Revier, Robert Edeson, Anders Randolt, Noah Beery.

One Night at Susie's—1930. First National. *Director:* John Francis Dillon. *Cast:* Billie Dove, Douglas Fairbanks, Jr., Helen Ware, Tully Marshall, J. Crane, John Loder.

Little Caesar—1931. Warner Bros. Released through First National. *Director:* Mervyn LeRoy. *Cast:* Edward G. Robinson, Douglas Fairbanks, Jr., Glenda Farrell, Sidney Blackmer, George E. Stone.

Chances—1931. Warner Bros. Released through First National. *Director:* Allan Dwan. *Cast:* Douglas Fairbanks, Jr., Anthony Bushell, Rose Hobart.

I Like Your Nerve—1931. Warner Bros. Released through First National. *Director:* William McGann. *Cast:* Douglas Fairbanks, Jr., Loretta Young, Henry Kolker, Boris Karloff, Claude Allister.

Union Depot—1931. Warner Bros. Released through First National.

Director: Alfred E. Green. *Cast:* Douglas Fairbanks, Jr., Joan Blondell, Guy Kibbee, Alan Hale, Frank McHugh.

It's Tough to Be Famous—1931. Warner Bros. Released through First National. *Director:* Alfred E. Green. *Cast:* Douglas Fairbanks, Jr., Mary Brian, Lillian Bond, Walter Catlett, Louise Beavers.

Love Is a Racket—1931. Warner Bros. Released through First National. *Director:* William A. Wellman. *Cast:* Douglas Fairbanks, Jr., Frances Dee, Lee Tracy, Lyle Talbot, Ann Dvorak.

Scarlet Dawn—1932. Warner Bros. Released through First National. *Director:* William Dieterle. *Cast:* Douglas Fairbanks, Jr., Nancy Carroll, Lilyan Tashman, Guy Kibbee.

Le Plombier Amoreux—1932. (**The Passionate Plumber**) MGM. *Director:* Claude Aurant-Lara. *Cast:* Buster Keaton, Jeannette Ferney, Douglas Fairbanks, Jr.

L'Athlete Malgre Lui—1932. Warner Bros. *Director:* Claude Autant-Lara. *Cast:* William Barry, Mathilde Comont, Carrie Daumery, George Davis, Jean Del Val, Jean Delmour, Douglas Fairbanks, Jr., Jeannette Ferney, Arthur Hurni, Barbara Leonard.

L'Aviateur—1932. Warner Bros. *Director:* John Daumery and William A. Seiter. *Writing:* James Montgomery (Play—*The Aviator*) Paul d'Estournelles de Constant. *Producer:* Irving Asher. *Cast:* André Cheron, Douglas Fairbanks, Jr., Jeanne Helbling, Leon Larive, Jacques Lory, Mireille (II), Rolla Norman, Geymond Vital.

Parachute Jumper—1933. Warner Bros. *Director:* Alfred E. Green.

Cast: Bette Davis, Douglas Fairbanks, Jr., Leo Carillo, Frank McHugh, Claire Dodd.

The Life of Jimmy Dolan—1933. Warner Bros. *Director:* Archie Mayo. *Cast:* Douglas Fairbanks, Jr., Loretta Young, Aline MacMahon, Lyle Talbot, Mickey Rooney, John Wayne, Guy Kibbee.

The Narrow Corner—1933. Warner Bros. *Director:* Alfred E. Green. *Cast:* Douglas Fairbanks, Jr., Patricia Ellis, Ralph Bellamy, Dudley Digges, Sidney Toler.

Captured—1933. Warner Bros. *Director:* Roy Del Ruth. *Cast:* Leslie Howard, Douglas Fairbanks, Jr., Paul Lukas, Margaret Lindsay, J. Carroll Naish.

Morning Glory—1933. RKO. *Director:* Lowell Sherman. *Cast:* Katharine Hepburn, Douglas Fairbanks, Jr., Adolphe Menjou, Mary Duncan, C. Aubrey Smith.

Catherine the Great—1934. London Films. Distributed through United Artists. *Director:* Paul Czinner. *Cast:* Douglas Fairbanks, Jr., Elisabeth Bergner, Flora Robson, Sir Gerald DuMaurier.

Success at Any Price—1934. (**Success Story**) RKO. *Director:* J. Walter Ruben. *Cast:* Colleen Moore, Douglas Fairbanks, Jr., Genevieve Tobin, Frank Morgan, Edward Everett Horton, Allen Vincent.

Mimi—1935. British International. Released through United Artists. *Director:* Paul Stein. *Cast:* Douglas Fairbanks, Jr., Gertrude Lawrence, Diana Napier, Harold Warrender, Carol Goodner.

Man of the Moment—1935. Warner Bros. *Director:* Monty Banks. Douglas Fairbanks, Jr., Laura LaPlante, Margaret Lockwood, Claude Hulbert, Donald Calthrop.

The Amateur Gentleman—1936. Criterion Films. (US Release United Artists.) *Director:* Thornton Freeland. *Cast:* Douglas Fairbanks, Jr., Elissa Landi, Gordon Harker, Margaret Lockwood, Hugh Williams, Basil Sydney, Irene Brown, Carol Brown, Athol Stewart, Esme Percy.

Accused—1936. Criterion Films. (US Release United Artists.) *Director:* Thornton Freeland. *Cast:* Douglas Fairbanks, Jr., Dolores del Rio, Florence Desmond, Basil Sydney, Cecil Humphreys, Esme Percy, Googie Withers, Roland Culver, Leo Genn.

When Thief Meets Thief—1937. Criterion Films-U.K. Released as **Jump for Glory**. (US Release United Artists.) *Director:* Raoul Walsh. *Cast:* Douglas Fairbanks, Jr., Valerie Hobson, Alan Hale, Jack Melford, Esme Percy, Leo Genn, Basil Radford.

The Prisoner of Zenda—1937. Selznick International. Released through United Artists. *Director:* John Cromwell. *Cast:* Ronald Colman, Madeleine Carroll, Douglas Fairbanks, Jr., Mary Astor, C. Aubrey Smith, Raymond Massey, David Niven.

The Joy of Living—1938. RKO. *Director:* Tay Garnett. *Cast:* Irene Dunne, Douglas Fairbanks, Jr., Alice Brady, Guy Kibbee, Jean Dixon, Eric Blore, Billy Gilbert, Franklin Pangborn, Lucille Ball.

The Rage of Paris—1938. Universal. *Director:* Henry Koster. *Cast:* Danielle Darneux, Douglas Fairbanks, Jr., Mischa Auer, Helen Broderick, Louis Hayward.

Having Wonderful Time—1938. RKO. *Director:* Alfred Santell. *Cast:* Ginger Rogers, Douglas

Fairbanks, Jr., Red Skelton, Lucille Ball, Eve Arden, Jack Carson, Donald Meek, Grady Sutton.

The Young in Heart—1938. United Artists. *Producer:* Selznick International. *Director:* Richard Wallace. *Cast:* Douglas Fairbanks, Jr., Janet Gaynor, Paulette Goddard, Roland Young, Billie Burke, Richard Carlson.

Gunga Din—1939. RKO. *Director:* George Stevens. *Cast:* Cary Grant, Victor McLaglen, Douglas Fairbanks, Jr., Sam Jaffe, Eduardo Ciannelli, Joan Fontaine, Robert Coote, Montagu Love.

The Sun Never Sets—1939. Universal. *Director:* Rowland V. Lee. *Cast:* Douglas Fairbanks, Jr., Basil Rathbone, Virginia Field, Lionel Atwill, Barbara O'Neil, C. Aubrey Smith.

Rulers of the Sea—1939. Paramount. *Director:* Frank Lloyd. *Cast:* Douglas Fairbanks, Jr., Margaret Lockwood, Will Fyffe, George Bancroft, Montagu Love.

Green Hell—1940. Universal. *Director:* James Whale. *Cast:* Douglas Fairbanks, Jr., Joan Bennett, John Howard, George Sanders, Vincent Price, Alan Hale, George Bancroft.

Safari—1940. Paramount. *Director:* Edward H. Griffith. *Cast:* Douglas Fairbanks, Jr., Madeleine Carroll, Tullio Carminati, Muriel Angelus, Lynne Overman, Billy Gilbert.

Angels Over Broadway—1940. Columbia. *Directors:* Ben Hecht and Lee Garmes. *Cast:* Douglas Fairbanks, Jr., Rita Hayworth, Thomas Mitchell, John Qualen, George Watts.

The Corsican Brothers—1941. Edward Small Productions. Released through United Artists. *Director:* Gregory Ratoff. *Cast:* Douglas Fairbanks, Jr.,

Akim Tainiroff, Ruth Warrick, J. Carroll Naish, H.B. Warner, John Emery, Henry Wilcoxon.

Sinbad the Sailor—1947. RKO. *Director:* Richard Wallace. *Cast:* Douglas Fairbanks, Jr., Maureen O'Hara, Anthony Quinn, Walter Slezak, George Tobias, Jane Greer, Mike Mazurki, Sheldon Leonard.

The Exile—1947. The Fairbanks Co./Universal-International. *Director:* Max Ophuls. *Cast:* Douglas Fairbanks, Jr., Paule Croset, Maria Montez, Nigel Bruce, Henry Daniell, Robert Coote.

That Lady in Ermine—1948. 20th Century–Fox. *Director:* Ernst Lubitsch/Otto Preminger. *Cast:* Betty Grable, Douglas Fairbanks, Jr., Cesar Romero, Walter Abel, Reginald Gardiner.

The Fighting O'Flynn—1949. Fairbanks Company/Universal-International. *Director:* Arthur Pierson. *Cast:* Douglas Fairbanks, Jr., Helena Carter, Richard Greene, Patricia Medina, Arthur Shields.

State Secret (The Great Manhunt)—1950. London Films. *Director:* Sidney Gilliat. *Cast:* Douglas Fairbanks, Jr., Glynis Johns, Jack Hawkins, Herbert Lom.

Mister Drake's Duck—1951. Angel Prod. *Director:* Val Guest. *Cast:* Douglas Fairbanks, Jr., Yolande Donlan, A.E. Matthews, Jon Pertwee, Wilfred Hyde-White.

Another Man's Poison—1952. Angel Prod. *Director:* Irving Rapper. *Cast:* Bette Davis, Douglas Fairbanks, Jr., Gary Merrill, Emlyn Williams.

Chase a Crooked Shadow—1958. Associated Dragon Prod. *Director:* Michael Anderson. *Cast:* Douglas Fairbanks, Jr., Richard Todd, Anne Baxter, Herbert Lom.

Francis Lederer

Francis Lederer certainly didn't *sound* like the elderly gentleman I was speaking to. His voice was strong with a charming accent, and his memory still vigorous at 96 years of age. He was born on November 6, 1899, in Prague, Czechoslovakia. Starting on the stage with the legendary director Max Reinhardt, soon he would find acclaim in the now classic film *Pandora's Box* (1929) under the direction of G.W. Pabst and starring an American icon, Louise Brooks.

Working on the stage was followed by film work with Germany's acclaimed UFA studios. At one time doing both, Francis, born Franz, was trained in all aspects of a classical actor. He would go on to make scores of films in America, where he first arrived in 1932.

ON STAGE WITH REINHARDT

"Under [Reinhardt's] direction I played Romeo in *Romeo and Juliet* [October 1928]. He was kind and brilliant, inspirational. Divine, divine, divine! It was just paradise. He not only directed me on stage, he took the trouble to have me come to his house, which was at that time a kind of a castle.

"He worked with me on the play word for word and took endless pains in pronunciation. He guided me in how to read those lines of Shakespeare and it was one of the highlights of my life. I finished *Romeo* on a Saturday, and on Monday I opened a musical in Berlin called *Die Wunderbar* and that was certainly a marvelous chance."

Lederer had originally sent a note to acclaimed German actress Elisabeth Bergner, who was currently playing Juliet, but in addition was seeking a new male star for her Romeo when the show was to go on tour. Not only did he get the audition, he was offered the role practically on the spot by Reinhardt.

After a much publicized "artistic feud" between Lederer's current producer in Berlin, Felix Saltenburg, whom he was under contract with, and Reinhardt, he was released and finally allowed to start rehearsals for a part that was pivotal in his career.

Lederer spoke of the experience in an article ("Max Reinhardt— The Starmaker") which came out in 1973 on the centennial celebration of the birth of Max Reinhardt. It is well worth repeating here for it sums up this monumental occasion.

"Reinhardt did not rehearse from ten to five as was the custom: he rehearsed literally day and night. I spent many a night at Max Reinhardt's home in Berlin, working with him and his assistants on my role. The dress rehearsal of *Romeo and Juliet*, the day before the opening, started at ten in the morning and lasted until three thirty the next morning. Incidentally, I had to get up at six that morning to work on a motion picture and so, with three hours' sleep, I went on stage that night playing Romeo for the first time. The rest became history. Reinhardt was acclaimed by all the critics as having discovered (and I am embarrassed to say it) the greatest Romeo of our time, and that label stuck with me, for in my next play, a musical called *Die Wunderbar*, I was still labeled as 'Our dancing and singing Romeo.'"

AFTER REINHARDT

I told Mr. Lederer that it was a thrill to be speaking to a legend. "Oh come on I'm not that," he modestly replied. But what *would* one call him? If he had done nothing but *Pandora's Box*, he would be emulated amidst the cinephiles of the world. But so much more: film upon film, stage works and teaching the art of acting to his present age!

"My first film that I made was called *Zuflucht* [1928]—it means 'Refuge.' It was with the greatest German motion picture star whose name was Henny Porten. I would say [with] my motion picture career I was extremely fortunate to have worked with people who are kind and experienced. I can only say the best about anything in my careers."

Francis Lederer's striking good looks certainly didn't hurt his career, either. When I suggested he was considered a matinee idol and a ladies' man he scoffed. "Those titles always made me embarrassed!"

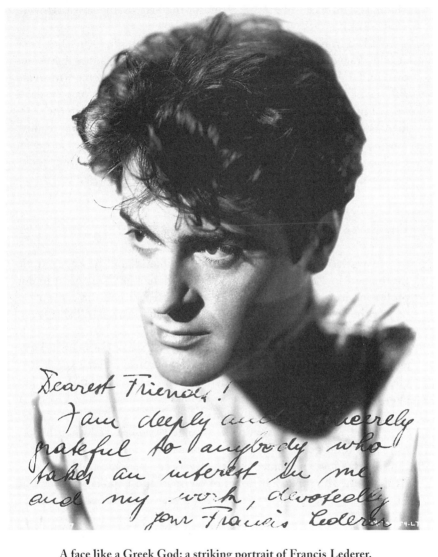

A face like a Greek God: a striking portrait of Francis Lederer.

Nonetheless, one can see why he would have indeed been considered an ideal Romeo for the Shakespeare classic.

Starting with Germany's acclaimed UFA Studio, Francis had caught the eye of director G.W. Pabst. Having first worked with Pabst on stage, his third film was also directed by him. *The Wonderful Lies of Nina Petrovna* (1929) also starred a superb and beautiful German actress, Brigitte

Helm. (Helm received great acclaim for the Fritz Lang classic *Metropolis* [1927].)

"I had worked with Pabst prior on the stage, in the Deutsches Theatre in Prague. It was a leading part, a marvelous part and a marvelous picture. UFA was a big, big company. I had some problems with *Nina Petrovna*. I had some eye problems because of the lighting for a few days.

"I had a scene in which I was a recruit, a young officer in the German army. The scene was shot in the opera and the particular leading actress, Brigitte Helm, sat in a box. My shot was looking up at her in the box and naturally, the *lights*. It hurt, I had to play the scene looking up at the high glaring lights. But it's all part of the game."

PANDORA'S BOX

"I was seen by G.W. Pabst, a great director, and he engaged me for the part in *Pandora's Box* [1929]. What makes anybody great in our profession is the *individuality*. The way that Pabst had the conception of *how* the actor should act. That is what makes stars. Mr. Pabst was a great director, a marvelous director.

"Louise Brooks was an *enigma!* She didn't speak German and was an American actress. I couldn't talk to her because I didn't speak English at the time! She had a gentleman with her, a translator with her who translated for her what the director Pabst meant. She had great individuality, a most unusual quality.

"She had a mystery about her. Strangely enough, I saw her the last time in a train going to Paris. Both of us had to make different pictures, it was just an accident that she was on the same train as I was. At that time she spoke a little bit of German and I spoke a little bit of English and that is how we conversed! It was an unforgettable experience.

"She had a quality about her that I call mysterious and she was a great actress; most unusual for an American actress. And this actor [Fritz] Kortner was marvelous in it."

In her autobiography *Lulu in Hollywood* Brooks herself recalled working with the German director who had united her and Lederer. "Silent film fans were excellent lip readers and often complained at the box office about the cowboy fussing furiously trying to mount his horse. Besides which, directors like Pabst used exact dialogue to isolate and intensify an emotion.

"When Lulu was looking down at the dead Schoen [Fritz Kortner], he gave me the line, 'Das Blut!' Not the murder of my husband but the sight of the *blood* determined the expression on my face."

And Franz Lederer was indeed lucky to have worked with Brooks. Very few films have inspired such countless articles and critiques on which has become unforgettable cinema. The potency of this film I liken to the first time I saw Josephine Baker's spectacular film. *Zou Zou* (1934). Sheer electricity, sheer magnetism. Lucky for all of us, *Pandora's Box* lives on as art, frame by glorious frame.

A somewhat perplexed Louise Brooks, who worked with Lederer in *Pandora's Box* (1929).

ACCLAIM ON BROADWAY

"In 1931 I went to London to do a play called *Meet My Sister*. I could not speak English at the time and I had to learn the whole part phonetically. I had a marvelous teacher in England. The play wasn't a big success and I was getting ready to go back to Berlin when the director met me back at the hotel. He said that a very interesting part was coming up and he thought I'd be right for it but the director was in Germany looking for an actor.

"So I stayed and met this new director, Basil Dean, and the play was *Autumn Crocus*. It was a huge success in London. The show was imported to Broadway in New York in 1932 where it was a highlight of the season. We toured also with the show and it was a triumph."

Triumph is an understatement. Lederer's performance was acclaimed by critics and audiences alike. For a Depression weary world of the 1930s, theater and cinema provided a well-needed escape from the realities of the bread lines. Lederer would never achieve such an extreme high in his career that could equal the success of *Autumn Crocus*.

Lederer with Fay Compton in the London production of *Autumn Crocus*, **April 1931.**

And because of his stage training and singing abilities, naturally Hollywood saw his extremely promising potential for films. His slight accent was thought to be a plus in ensuring an already charismatic pull with his good looks and innate sexuality on the stage.

New York audiences could not get enough of Lederer. When the play opened, none other than the great George M. Cohan himself was quoted in the *New York Times* on November 29, 1932. "A real actor, this kid, Francis Lederer. He'll tear your heart out when he starts to emote. 'Autumn Crocus' should prove a big success."

Extra matinee performances had to be added on every Thursday to accommodate the theater crowd. Lederer had indeed arrived. Critics outdid themselves in coining platitudes for Lederer. In the January 1933 issue of *Vanity Fair* magazine, it was noted that "Francis Lederer was Lee Shubert's Christmas gift to the women of America, and ever since he made his debut here in *Autumn Crocus* the feminine hearts of the nation have beat, not in waltz-time, but in a frenetic polka."

Lederer did not like being considered a "matinee idol." When I suggested this title which had been thrust on him, he was quick to respond. "Please! I don't contribute that to me. That was the critics. Those titles always embarrassed me." Nonetheless, his extreme good looks and winning personality lay this wreath about his head. Clearly he would have preferred further exploration into the art of the theater.

The *New York World Telegram*'s critic Heywood Broun reported Lederer's arrival on the New York stage with glee on November 21, 1932. Broun wrote that "One industry which was languishing revived mightily last Saturday night. There has been very little going on in the matter of matinee-idoling hereabouts of late. Matinees themselves have seemed at the point of death, let alone matinee idols. And suddenly there stepped upon the stage a young Czech whose name is Francis Lederer. To these old ears there came a sound which has been long denied them. It is compounded out of 'oh' and 'ah' and of soprano quality."

New York Post writer John Mason Brown wrote the following on December 12, 1932: "Though it is probably the last thing in the world he wants from anybody, still I must confess that Mr. Francis Lederer has my sympathy. He has won it because to the majority of playgoers in this town (which is only another way of saying the "ladies") he has become the active embodiment of a long extinct tradition. In other words, it is his misfortune to have had thrust upon him overnight a reputation as a matinee idol."

ASSIGNMENT: HOLLYWOOD

Lederer not only had once again conquered the legitimate stage, he also had signed a contract with RKO Studios where he would begin his film career in America. *Screenland Magazine*'s "Honor Page" went to Lederer in December 1934. "A new idol has come to dwell amongst us! Not since Chevalier first enchanted us with his European gaiety have we had such a heart-warming occasion for tossing our editorial hat in the air in tribute to a blithe spirit, bringing a freshness and a romantic joyousness to our hungry screens."

Going from the legitimate stage to silent films and then to talking pictures must have seemed a natural succession for Lederer. "You are talking to a person who was blessed [with] experiences in the motion picture and stage business.

"I would say in my motion picture career I was extremely fortunate to have worked with motion picture people who [were] kind and

The Man I Married, 1940, 20th Century–Fox: Lederer and Joan Bennett (courtesy of Rozella Renish).

Confessions of a Nazi Spy, 1939, Warner Bros.: Lederer with Edward G. Robinson (courtesy of Rozella Renish).

experienced. I can only say the best about anything in my career. I had first started naturally, in silent pictures and then talking pictures in Germany and then in England and Hollywood afterwards.

"Naturally all actors from stage prefer talking pictures but it was easier in *silents* [because] I didn't have to learn the English language. I enjoyed all the pictures I made that were good in script. Sometimes I made a mistake in picking something that was not really right. I did it and I regretted it."

As Lederer's film career expanded, naturally the opportunity for working and meeting with other major stars occurred. He spoke on some of these screen legends and the impact they had on his own career.

"Well to work with such people as John Barrymore ... he was absolutely fantastic. I remember him walking down the stairs at a party.

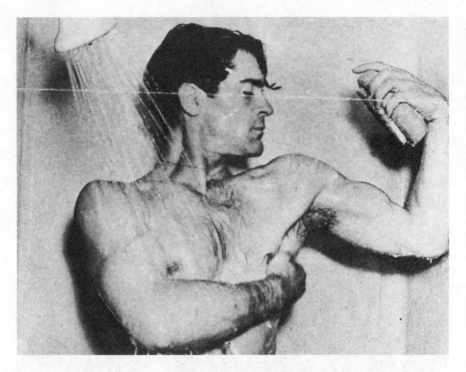

Francis Lederer flexing those pecs, 1930s style.

He was an individual as you don't find them. He was just *Barrymore*, unusual quality.

"I was given the Mary Pickford Lifetime Achievement Award by Pickford. She was kind, warm and just charming. She was wonderful to me. And Ida Lupino was a darling, I made a picture with her.

"Adolphe Menjou was a very, very encouraging, brilliant and fascinating man. I had known Emil Jannings but I didn't work with him. He was the greatest German actor. And I was fortunate to have Pola Negri and Ernst Lubitsch as friends.

"I only saw Marlene Dietrich on stage. I never worked with her but she just stuck out in the production that she did in Berlin and we became friends. She was beautiful, she was brilliant. From the stage, that's how she got into pictures. [Dietrich also started in Berlin doing stage work with Max Reinhardt. Her film *The Blue Angel* (1930) brought Dietrich international acclaim.]

"I did three one act plays with Gloria Swanson. She was an excellent actress and I enjoyed it tremendously. I was very fortunate."

My American Wife, 1936, Paramount: Francis Lederer with Ann Sothern (courtesy of Rozella Renish).

LIFE TODAY

When this book goes to press, Francis Lederer will have celebrated his 99th birthday. He lives in Canoga Park, California, with his third wife Marion. She was equally as gracious and kind when we spoke, and after 56 years of marriage to Lederer, Marion was as proud of his accomplishments as Francis.

First married to opera singer Ada Nejedly in Prague, Lederer went on to marry actress Margo and now Marion Irvine. "We were married in 1941," said Marion. "Margo married Eddie Albert ... and we were good friends."

What struck me most immediately was Lederer's extreme humility. He was genuinely surprised that someone would *want* to take so much time with this interview. Lederer still teaches at the acting school he founded in 1956, the American National Academy of Performing Arts in Hollywood.

"I started it with children and it became an academy. We teach ballet and modern jazz, tap dancing and every aspect of what belongs to our profession. I teach acting, and as Leonardo da Vinci said, 'Through teaching I have learned.'"

I ask him if his students knew what a great legend they were working with and he laughed. "I don't think so." And for some peculiar reason, Lederer's film career didn't reach the heights that it was expected to. Although when one looks at the list of films he made with diverse stories and co-stars, it is indeed perplexing.

And how, I ask, would he like to be remembered? "I don't care about giving that a thought," he chuckled. "I would be grateful if they do [remember me]. I guess it is just, you know, that you are lucky to have been in those pictures when your primary interest is in motion pictures."

FILMOGRAPHY

Zuflucht—1928. UFA Studios, Germany. *Cinematography:* Gustave Preiss. *Writing Credits:* Friedrich Raff. *Director:* Carl Froelich. *Cast:* Rudolf Biebrach, Bodo Bronsky, Carl De Vogt, Francis Lederer, Max Maximilian, Henny Porten, Lotte Stein.

Die Büchse der Pandora (Pandora's Box)—1928. (Also known as **Lulu.**) UFA Studios, Germany. *Writing Credits:* Joseph Fleisler and Georg Wilhelm Pabst. *Cast:* Louise Brooks, Fritz Kortner, Carl Goetz, Alice Roberts, Daisy D'ora, Krafft Raschig, Sig Arno, Michael von Newlinsky, Gustav Diessl, Francis Lederer.

Die Wunderbare Lüge der Nina Petrowna—1929. Nero Films (**The Wonderful Lies of Nina Petrovna**). UFA Studios. *Writing Credits:* Hans Szekely. *Director:* Hanns Schwarz. *Producer:* Erich Pommer. *Cinematography:* Carl Hoffmann. *Art Director:* Robert Herlth, Walter Rohrig. *Cast:* Ekkehard Arendt, Harry Hardt, Brigitte Helm, Lya Jan, Francis Lederer, Michael von Newlinsky.

Meineid—1929. Nero Films. *Director:* Georg Jacoby. *Writing Credits:* Herbert Juttke, Jeorg C. Klaren. *Cinematography:* Willie Goldberger. *Cast:* Carl Auen, Gerd Briese, Paul Henckels, La Jana, Inge Landgutt, Francis Lederer, Miles Mander, Alice Roberte.

Atlantic—1929. British International Pictures. *Director:* Ewald Andre Dupont. *Writing Credits:* Ewald Andre Dupont, Victor Kendall, Ernest Raymond. *Cinematography:* Charles Rosher. *Cast:* Fritz Kortner, Elsa Wagner, Heinrich, Schroth, Julia Serda, Elfriede Borodin, Lucie Mannheim, Francis Lederer, Willi Forst, Hermann Vallentin, Theodor Loos, Georg John, Philipp Manning, Georg August Koch, Syd Crossley.

Maman Colibri—1929. *Director:* Julien Duvivier. *Writing Credit:* Julien Duvivier (known as **Mother Hummingbird** in USA). *Cast:* Jeanne Dax, Jean Gerard, Helene Hallier, Maria Jacobini, Francis Lederer.

Ihre Majestät die Liebe—1930. UFA Studio. *Director:* Joseph Mandel (Joe May). *Cast:* Kurt Gerron, Francis Lederer, Kathe von Nagy.

Die Große Sehnsucht—1930. UFA Studio. *Director:* Istvan Szekely. *Writing Credits:* Emeric Pressburger, Istvan Szekely. *Music:* Karl Brull, Paul Dessau, Rudolf Eisner. *Cinematography:* Mutz Greenbaum. *Cast:* betty Amann, Ferdinand Bonn, Elga Brink, Lil Dagover, Gustav Diessl, Harry Frank, Irma Godau, Liane Haid, Paul Heidemann, Paul Henckels, Camilla Horn, Walter Janssen, Paul Kemp (I), Fritz Kortner, Francis Lederer, Harry Liedtke, Theo Lingen, Theodor Loos, Anna Muller-Lincke, Anny Ondra, Berthe Ostyn, Maria Paudler, Karl Platen, Charles Puffy, Fritz Rasp, Walter Rilla, Adele Sandrock, Wilhelmine Sandrock, Hans Adalbert Schlettow, Walter Steinbeck, Jack Trevor Story, Charlotte Susa, Luis Trenker, Olga Tschechowa, Conrad Veidt, Ernst Verebes, Erwin van Roy, Camilla von Hollay.

Man of Two Worlds—1934. RKO Radio Pictures, Inc. A Pandro S Berman Production. *Distributor:* RKO Radio Pictures, Inc. B&W. 10 reels. 92 min. Passed by the National Board of Review. *Executive Producer:* Merian C. Cooper. *Director:* J. Walter Ruben. *Assistant Director:* Jimmy Anderson. *Script:* Howard J. Green and Ainsworth Morgan. *Photography:* Henry W. Gerrard. *Photography effects:* Vernon

Walker. *Art Director:* Van Nest Polglase and Al Herman. *Editor:* Jack Hively. *Production Editor:* George Hively. *Musical Director:* Max Steiner. *Recording:* John Tribby. *Techical Advisor:* Capt. Frank E. Kleinschmidt. *Cast:* Francis Lederer, Elissa Landi, Henry Stephenson, J. Farrell MacDonald, Steffi Duna, Sarah Padden, Walter Bryon, Forrester Harvey, Ivan Simpson, Lumsden Hare, Christian Rub, Emil Chautard, Gertrude Wise.

The Pursuit of Happiness—1934. Paramount Productions, Inc. *Distributor:* Paramount Productions, Inc. *Sound:* (Western Electric Noiseless Recording). B&W. 8 reels. 80, 83 or 85 min. Passed by the National Board of Review. *Presented by:* Adolph Zukor. *Producer:* Arthur Hornblow, Jr. *Executive Producer:* Emanuel Coh. *Director:* Alexander Hall. *Assistant Director:* Ewing Scott. *Script:* J.P. McEvoy and Virginia Van Upp. *Adaptation:* Stephen Morehouse, Avery and Jack Cunningham. *Photography:* Karl Struss. *Art Director:* Hans Dreier and Bernard Herzbrun. *Cast:* Francis Lederer, Joan Bennett, Charlie Ruggles, Mary Boland, Walter Kingsford, Minor Watson, Adrian Morris, Barbara Barondess, Duke York, Burr Caruth, Jules Cowles, Irving Bacon, Spencer Charters, John Marston, Henry Mowbray, Boyd Irwin, Holmes Herbert, Colin Tapley, Bert Sprotte, Reginald Pasch, Edward Peil, Sr., Harry Schultz, Paul Kruger, Winter Hall, Hans Von Morhart, Baron Hesse, George Billings, Ricca Allen.

The Gay Deception—1935. Fox Film Corp. Jesse L. Lasky Productions. *Distributor:* Twentieth Century–Fox Film Corp. B&W. 9 reels. 6,906 feet. 75–76 min. *Director:* William Wyler. *Assistant Director:* Ad Schaumer. *Original Script:* Stephen Avery and Don Hartman. *Photographer:* Joseph Valentine. *Musical Director:* Louis DeFrancesco. *Cast:* Francis Lederer, Frances Dee, Benita Hume, Alan Mowbray, Lennox Pawle, Adele St. Maur, Akim Tamiroff, Luis Alberni, Lionel Stander, Ferdinand Gottschalk, Richard Carle, Lenita Lane, Barbara Fritchie, Paul Hurst, Robert Greig, Funner Paulson, Rudolf Myzet Maidel Turner, John T. Murray, Frank Melton, Fred Wallace, William Stelling, Fred Sylva, Vic Chatten, Walter Lawrence, David O'Brien, Charles Sellon, Jane Barnes, Ruth Warren, Rita Owin, Mary Akin, Doro Merande, Anne O'Neal, Robert Graves, Francis Sayles, Gus Reed, Jack Mulhall, Spencer Charters, Paul McVey, Lew Kelly, Torben Meyer, Hector V. Sarno, Neal Burns, Olaf Hytten, Thomas Pogue, Phil Tead, Billy Wayne, Jack Hatfield, Agostino Borgato, George Humbert, Alan Bridge, Wade Boteler, Russ Clark, Rodney Hildebrand, Jack Mower, Brady Kline, Esther Muir, Iris Adrian, Paul Irving, Maidena Armstrong, Eddie Fetherston, Nell Craig, Sam Ash.

Romance in Manhattan—1935. RKO Radio Pictures, Inc. A Pandro S. Berman Production. *Distributor:* RKO Radio Pictures, Inc. *Sound:* (RCA Photophone System). B&W. 8 reels. 75 or 78 min.

Director: Stephen Roberts. *Assistant Director:* Dewey Starkey. *Script:* Jane Murfin and Edward Kaufman. *Story:* Norman Krasna and Don Hartman. *Photography:* Nick Musuraca. *Music Director:* Al Colombo. *Cast:* Francis Lederer, Ginger Rogers, Arthur Hohl, Jimmy Butler, J. Farrell MacDonald, Helen Ware, Eily Malyon, Lillian Harmer, Donald Meek, Sidney Toler, Ascar Apfel, Reginald Barlow, Guinn Williams, Harold Goodwin, Spencer Charters.

My American Wife—1936. Paramount Productions, Inc. *Distributor:* Paramount Productions, Inc. B&W. 8 reels. 65, 70 or 75 min. Passed by the National Board of Review. *Executive Producer:* William LeBaron. *Director:* Harold Young. *Assistant Director:* Richard Harlan. *Script:* Virginia Van Upp. *Photography:* Harry Fischbeck. *Art Director:* Hans Dreir and Robert Odell. *Cast:* Francis Lederer, Ann Sothern, Fred Stone, Billie Burke, Ernest Cossart, Grant Mitchell, Hal K. Dawson, Helene Millard, Elsie Clark, Buck Connors, Dale Armstrong, Noble Johnson, Henry Roquemore, Eddie Dunn, Jimmy Vandiveer, Frank Marlowe, Don Brodie, Art Rowlands, Jim Toney, Ernie Adams, Isabelle LaMore, Nina Borget, Nenette Lafayette, Florence Wix, Phillip Smalley, Billy Gilbert, Margaret Brayton, Heinie Conklin, Doodles Weaver, Leonard Trainor, George Guhl, Spencer Charters, Dorothy Tennant, Edwin Stanley, Sarah Edwards.

One Rainy Afternoon—1936. Pickford-Lasky Productions, Inc. *Distributor:* United Artists Productions, Inc., United Artists Corp. B&W. 75 or 79–80. *Director:* Rowland V. Lee. *Assistant Director:* Percy Ikerd. *Photography:* Peverell Marley and Merritt Gerstad. *Cast:* Francis Lederer, Ida Lupino, Hugh Herbert, Roland Young, Erik Rhodes, Joseph Cawthorn, Countess Liev de Maigret, Donald Meek, Georgia Caine, Murray Kinell, Mischa Auer, Richard Carle, Phyllis Barry, Lois January, Eily Malyon, Seger Ellis, Margaret Warner, Lucille Ward, Angie Norton, Emilie Cabanne, Ferdinand Munier, Paul Irving, Billy Gilbert, Harvey Clark.

It's All Yours—1937. Columbia Pictures Corp of California, Ltd. *Distributor:* Columbia Pictures Corp. of California. B&W. 8 reels. 59, 77 or 80 min. *Producer:* William Perlberg. *Director:* Elliott Nugent. *Assistant Director:* Cliff Broughton. *Photography:* Henry Freulich. *Art Director:* Stephen Goosson. *Film Editor:* Gene Havlick. *Cast:* Madeleine Carroll, Francis Lederer, Mischa Auer, Grace Bradley, Victor Kilian, George McKay, Charles Waldron, J.C. Nugent, Richard Carle, Arthur Hoyt, Franklin Pangborn, Gene Morgan, Walter Anthony Merrill, Boyd Irwin Sr., C. Montague Shaw, Matt McHugh, Scott Colton, Lee Prather, Lucille Ward, Beatrice Curtis, Ruth Hilliard, Larry Wheat, Vesey O'Davoren, Phyllis Godfrey, Gertrude Webber, Eddie Laughton, Maurice Brierre, Ann Doran, Carli Taylor, Harry Hollingsworth, E.L. Dale, Louise Stanley, Antrim Short, Edmund Cobb, Leser Dorr, Don Marion,

John Rand, Connie Boswell, Michael Breen.

The Lone Wolf in Paris—1938. Columbia Pictures Corp of California, Ltd. *Distributor:* Columbia Pictures Corp. of California. B&W. 7 reels. 66–67 min. *Executive Producer:* Irving Briskin. *Associate Producer:* Wallace MacDonald. *Director:* Albert S. Rogell. *Assistant Director:* Clifford Broughton. *Photography:* Lucien Ballard. *Music Director:* Morris Stoloff. *Cast:* Francis Lederer, Frances Drake, Olaf Hytten, Walter Kingsford, Leona Maricle, Albert Van Dekker, Maurice Cass, Bess Flowers, Ruth Robinson, Pio Peretti, Eddie Fetherston, Otto Fries, Roger Gray, George Andre Beranger, Vernon Dent, Dick Curtis, Lucille Ward, Aileen Carlyle, Eugene Borden, Al Herman, Frank Leigh.

Midnight—1939. Paramount Pictures, Inc. B&W. 10 reels. 8,429 feet. 94 min. *Director:* Mitchell Leisen. *Assistant Director* and *Second Unit Director:* Hal Walker. *Script:* Charles Brackett and Billy Wilder. *Story:* Edwin Justus Mayer and Frank Schulz. *Photography:* Charles Lang, Jr. *Original Score:* Frederick Hollander. *Cast:* Claudette Colbert, Don Ameche, John Barrymore, Francis Lederer, Mary Astor, Elaine Barrie, Hedda Hopper, Rex O'Malley, Monty Woolley, Armand Kaliz, Lionel Pape, Ferdinand Munier, Gernnaro Curci.

Confessions of a Nazi Spy—1939. Warner Bros Pictures, Inc. A First National Picture. *Distributor:* Warner Bros Pictures, Inc. B&W. 11 reels. 102 or 110 min. *Executive*

Producers: Jack L. Warner and Hal B. Wallis. *Director:* Anatole Litvak. *Music Director:* Leo F. Forbstein. *Cast:* Edward G. Robinson, Francis Lederer, George Sanders, Paul Lukas, Henry O'Neill, Dorothy Tree, Lya Lys, Grace Stafford, James Stephenson, Celia Sibelius, Joe Sawyer, Sig Rumann, Lionel Royce, Henry Victor, Hans von Twardowsky, John Voigt, Frederick Vogeding, Willy Kaufman, Robert Davis, William Vaughn, George Rosener, Frederick Burton, Ely Malyon, Bodil Rosing, Fred Tozere, Frank Mayo, Lucien Prival, Martin Kosleck, Ward Bond, Alec Craig, Jack Mower, Jean Brooks, Robert Emmett Kean, Charles Sherlock, Edward Keane, William Gould, John Hamilton, Selmer Jackson, Emmett Vogan, John Ridgely, Egon Brecher, Edwin Stanley, Niccolai Yoshkin, John Conte, Charles Trowbridge, Tommy Bupp, Ferdinand Schumann-Heink.

The Man I Married—1940. Twentieth Century–Fox Film Corp. B&W. 6,940 feet. 65 or 76-77 min. *Producer:* Darryll F. Zanuck. *Director:* Irving Pichel. *Director of Photography:* Peverell Marley. *Music Director:* David Buffolph. *Cast:* Joan Bennett, Francis Lederer, Lloyd Nolan, Anna Sten, Otto Kruger, Maria Ouspenskaya, Ludwig Stossel, Johnny Russell, Lionel Royce, Fredrik Vogeding, Ernst Deutsch, Egon Brecher,William Kaufman, Frank Reicher, Charles Irwin, Lillian Porter, Lillian West, Hans Von Morhart, William Yetter, Carl Freybe, Ragnar Qvale, Rudy Frolich, John Start, Tom Mizer, Hans Schumm, Robert O.

Davis, Greta Meyer, Albert Geigel, Eleanor Wesselhoeft, Diane Fisher, John Hiestand, Leyland Hodgson, Arno Frey, Eugene Borden, Harry Depp.

Puddin' Head—1941. Republic Pictures. *Director:* Joseph Santley. *Writing Credits:* Milt Gross, Howard Snyder, Jack Townley, Hugh Wedlock Jr. *Producer:* Albert J. Cohen. *Cinematography:* Jack A. Marta. *Music Director:* Cy Feuer. *Cast:* Astrid Allwyn, Vince Barnett, Judy Canova, Chick Chandler, Eddie Foy Jr., Paul Harvey, Alma Kruger, Nora Lane, Francis Lederer, Wendell Niles, Hugh O'Connell, Gerald Oliver Smith. Slim Summerville, Raymond Walburn.

A Voice in the Wind—1944. United Artists. *Director:* Arthur Ripley. *Writing Credit:* Arthur Ripley. *Music:* Michel Michelet. *Cinematography:* Richard Fryer. *Cast:* Luis Alberni, J. Edward Bromberg, David Cota, Olga Fabian, Alexander Granach, Sigrid Gurie, Francis Lederer, J. Carroll Naish, Hans Schumm.

The Bridge of San Luis Rey—1944. United Artists. *Director:* Roland V. Lee. *Writing Credits:* Howard Estabrook, Herman Weissman, Thorton Wilder. *Music:* Dimitri Tiomkin. *Cinematography:* John W. Boyle. *Cast:* Lynn Bari, Akim Tamiroff, Francis Lederer, Alla Nazimova, Louis Calhern, Blanche Yurka, Donald Woods, Emma Dunn, Barton Hepburn, Joan Lorring, Abner Biberman, Minerva Urecal.

The Madonna's Secret—1946. Republic Pictures. *Director:* Wilhelm Thiele. *Writing Credits:* Brad-bury Foote, Wilhelm Thiele. *Music:* Joseph Dubin. *Cinematography:* John Alton. *Cast:* Edward Ashley, Clifford Brooke, John Hamilton, Michael Hawkes, Francis Lederer, John Litel, Gail Patrick, Leona Roberts, Ann Rutherford, Linda Stirling, Geraldine Wall, Pierre Watkin, Will Wright.

The Diary of a Chambermaid—1946. Camden Productions. *Distributor:* United Artists. *Director:* Jean Renoir. *Writing Credits:* Andre De Lorde, Andre Heuse, Burgess Meredith, Octave Mirbeau, Thielly Nores. *Music:* Michel Michelet. *Cinematography:* Lucien N. Andriot. *Cast:* Paulette Goddard, Burgess Meredith, Hurd Hatfield, Francis Lederer, Judith Anderson, Florence Bates, Irene Ryan, Reginald Owen, Almira Sessions.

Million Dollar Weekend—1948. Eagle-Lion Films. *Director:* Gene Raymond. *Writing Credit:* Charles Belden. *Music:* Phil Ohman. *Cinematography:* Paul Ivano. *Cast:* James Craven, Francis Lederer, Osa Massen, Stephanie Paull, Gene Raymond, Patricia Shay, Robert Warwick.

Captain Carey, U.S.A.—1950. Paramount. *Director:* Mitchell Leisen. *Writing Credits:* Martha Albrand, Robert Thoeren (also known as **After Midnight**). *Cast:* Alan Ladd, Wanda Hendrix, Francis Lederer, Joseph Calleia, Celia Lovsky, Richard Avonde, Frank Puglia, Luis Alberni, Angela Clarke, Roland Winters, Paul Lees, Jane Nigh, Russ Tamblyn, Virginia Farmer, David Leonard.

Surrender—1950. Republic Pictures. *Director:* Allan Dwan. *Writing*

Credits: James Edward Grant, Sloan Nibley. *Music:* Nathan Scott. *Cast:* Shelby Bacon, Roy Barcroft, Walter Brennan, Norman Budd, John Carroll, Howland Chamberlain, William Ching, Doris Cole, Frank Dae, Esther Dale, Jane Darwell, Kenne Duncan, Ralph Dunn, Elizabeth Dunne, Cecil Elliott, Dick Elliott, Virginia Farmer, Paul Fix Nacho Galindo, Fred Hoose, Wesley Hopper, J. Louis Johnson, Francis Lederer, Tina Menard, Charles Morton, Al Murphy, Edward Norris, Maria Palmer, Vera Ralston, Al Rhein, Tony Roux, Petra Silva, Mickey Simpson, Paul Stader, Glenn Strange, Tex Terry, Jeff York.

A Woman of Distinction—1950. Columbia Pictures Corp. *Director:* Edward Buzzell. *Writing Credits:* Hugo Butler, Charles Hoffman, Ian McLellan Hunter, Frank Tashlin. *Cast:* Rosalind Russell, Ray Milland, Edmund Gwenn, Janis Carter, Mary Jane Saunders, Francis Lederer, Jerome Courtland, Lucille Ball, Richard Bartell, Larry Barton, Marie Blake, Gail Bonney, Al Bridge, Lucille Browne, Harry Cheshire, Dudley Dickerson, Charles Evans, Elizabeth Flourney, Maxine Gates, Alex Gerry, Gale Gordon, William E. Green, Lois Hall, Harry Harvey, Jr., Myron Healey, Charles Jordan, Ted Jordan, Edward Keane, Donald Kerr, Robert Malcolm, Wanda McKay, Mira McKinney, Billy Newell, Walter Sande, John Smith, Harry Strang, Aline Towne, Charles Trowbridge, Harry Tyler, Lelah Tyler, Napoleon Whiting, Jean Willes, Charlotte Wynters, Clifton Young.

Abenteuer in Wien—1952. Schonbrunn-Film. *Director:* Emile Reinert (Austria). *Writing Credits:* Michael Kehlmann, Franz Tassie. *Cast:* Gustav Frolich, Adrienne Gessner, Inge Konradi, Francis Lederer, Guido Wieland, Egon von Jordan.

Stolen Identity—1953. Helen Ainsworth Corp. (US). *Director:* Gunther von Fritsch. *Writing Credits:* Robert Hill, Alexander Lernet-Holenia. *Music:* Richard Hageman. *Cinematography:* Helmut Ashley. *Cast:* Donald Buka, Joan Camden, Francis Lederer, Egon von Jordan, Inge Konradi, Hermann Erhardt, Turhan Bey, Adrienne Gessner, Manfred Inger, Gisela Wilke.

Lisbon—1956. Republic Pictures. *Director:* Ray Milland. *Writing Credits:* John Tucker Battle, Martin Rackin. *Music:* Nelson Riddle. *Cinematography:* Jack A. Marta. *Cast:* Ray Milland, Maureen O'Hara, Claude Rains, Yvonne Furneaux, Francis Lederer, Percy Marmont, J. Novello, Edward Chapmin, Harold Jamieson.

The Ambassador's Daughter—1956. United Artists. *Director:* Norman Krasna. *Writing Credits:* Norman Krasna. *Music:* Jacques Metehen. *Cinematography:* Michel Kelber. *Cast:* Oliva de Havilland, John Forsythe, Myrna Loy, Adolphe Menjou, Tommy Noonan, Francis Lederer, Edward Arnold, Minor Watson.

Maracaibo—1958. *Director:* Cornell Wilde. *Writing Credits:* Ted Sherdeman, Stirling Silliphant. *Cast:* Michael Landon, Francis Lederer, Jean Wallace, Cornell Wilde.

The Return of Dracula—1958. Gramercy Pictures/United Artists. *Director:* Paul Landres. *Writing Credit:* Pat Fielder. *Music:* Gerald Fried. *Cinematography:* Jack Mac Kenzie. *Cast:* Francis Lederer, Norma Eberhardt, Ray Stricklyn, John Wengraf, Virginia Vincent, Gage Clarke, Jimmy Vaird, Greta Granstedt, Enid Yousen. Mel Allen, William Fawcett, Joseph Hamilton, Harry Harvey, Robert Lynn, John McNamara, Norbert Chiller, Charles Tannen.

Terror Is a Man—1959. Lynn-Romero Productions/Premiere Productions. *Director:* Gerardo de Leon. *Writing Credits:* Harry Paul Harber, H.G. Wells (novel: *The Island of Dr. Moreau*). *Music:* Ariston Auelino. *Cinematography:* Emmanuel I. Rojas. *Cast:* Francis Lederer, Greta Thyssen, Richard Derr, Oscar Keesee, Jr., Lilio Duran, Peyton Keesee, Flory Carlos.

Molly O'Day

Obtaining an interview with Molly O'Day wasn't an easy task. Looking back, I could probably have wallpapered my bedroom with the number of postage stamps which adorned her letters! Success finally was achieved, and when I heard from her daughter Ginny, I pleaded with her to set something up with her mom.

"You know," she said, "she really didn't have that long of a career in films. She more or less feels that part of her life is ancient history." Ginny and I talked about Molly's career and she agreed to help me as best she could. I assured her that her mom held a vital role in the silent film era. If she had made no films other than *The Patent Leather Kid* (1927), she would have maintained her legacy in silent films.

She was born Suzanne Noonan in October 1910 in Bayonne, New Jersey. (Miss O'Day passed away October 15, 1998.) One of eleven children, Molly and her siblings were raised by a devoted mother, Hannah, who loved the opera. "She had a beautiful singing voice. She was never a professional singer but she did have a beautiful singing voice."

Molly's father was Judge Thomas Francis Noonan, and after his death, money apparently became a concern for the family. The Noonan family sold their home and moved to California. According to Molly, "The banks closed and we became poor. I was fourteen, lived in California, so tried for acting in the movies. Luckily I was a success. I was pretty, a fresh face, so it all took off and started a career."

Sister acts abounded during the silent film era: Lillian and Dorothy Gish, Constance and Norma Talmadge, Priscilla and Marjorie Bonner, Loretta Young and Sally Blane and the Duncan Sisters to name but a

It's Official! Molly's a Star!" On the cover of *Motion Picture* magazine, July 1928.

Molly O'Day in 1927.

few. So it was with the Noonan girls. Molly's sisters Sally O'Neil and Isabelle both entered movies.

Sister Sally had, perhaps, the longest film career and received her big break with *Sally, Irene, and Mary* (1925). Virginia Noonan became Sally O'Neil on the advice of MGM. And First National eventually changed Suzanne Noonan's name to Molly O'Day. Isabelle eventually realized films were not for her and bowed out, leaving Molly and Sally to achieve stardom.

Child star Frank "Junior" Coghlan remembers the Noonan family. "I worked with Sally O'Neil in both *Mike* [1926] and *Slide, Kelly, Slide* [1927]. I never worked with Molly O'Day, but the Noonan family, their real name, were next door neighbors of ours for several years in the mid–1920s. As to what they were like? Well I was only a kid, but really liked both of the sisters very much. Having worked with Sally twice, I of course knew her much better than Molly."

STARTING WITH HAL ROACH

Molly started her career making two reelers with Hal Roach. With him, she quickly learned "the basics of being filmed, what to do, what not." She also remembered making independent films with Buster Keaton, one of the masters of cinema comedy.

"What a sweet, wholesome man! We were both on location and that's how it came about. He was a very individual person and very sweet. I enjoyed working with him very much. I didn't meet Chaplin [but] I had met Harold Lloyd, very nice, very real. I knew Loretta [Young] and her sister Sally [Blane] quite well. We went to the same Catholic girls high school together.

"Rudolph Valentino was way before my time. I never met him or Garbo. They were European and the Europeans and the Americans didn't get together that often. I think the [cultural differences] had a lot to do with it."

Much play was given to Molly's Irish heritage. *Screenland Magazine*'s July 1927 issue noted that "when Molly O'Day smiles, your own heart skips a beat and you look into a pair of hazel eyes, fringed with long dark lashes and reflect that if Ireland never produced anything but lovely women it would merit a place in the sun."

THE LUCK 'O THE IRISH

Molly's big break occurred when she went on a casting call to First National for the role of Curley Callahan in *The Patent Leather Kid* (1927). She was literally up against hundreds of hopefuls including Fox star Sally Eilers. Molly won this coveted role which pole-vaulted her to stardom.

Richard Barthelmess was already a major star when he took on the role of the prize fighter in the film. Molly O'Day recalled her deep admiration for him as well as director Al Santell.

"Well it was very wonderful because he [Barthelmess] was a seasoned performer and he could teach me an awful lot and he did teach me an awful lot. Mr. Barthelmess was a delight to work with, very helpful. He took me under his wing, so to speak. I was quite young and had rather a 'crush' on him. He was a handsome, established star and I was to play opposite him!

Molly O'Day and Richard Barthelmess in *Patent Leather Kid* (1927).

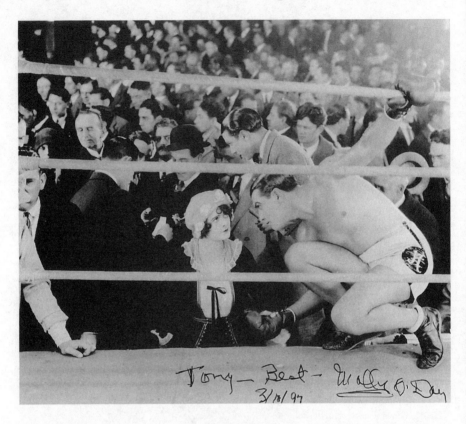

O'Day with her favorite actor, Richard Barthelmess, in *Patent Leather Kid.*

"We did one other film together, *The Little Shepherd of Kingdom Come* [1928]. I liked [director] Al Santell very much. He had great depth and great understanding [which] I felt would be important."

But it was her role in *The Patent Leather Kid* that drew much praise for the young actress. *New York Times* film critic Mordaunt Hall praised her performance: "Miss O'Day, who has only been seen in two reel subjects, is a sister of Sally O'Neil. Her acting in this tale rivals that of Mr. Barthelmess. She is sincere and earnest, whether it is when she becomes a nurse or when she is a dancer in a rough and tumble hall. She has beautiful large eyes and a retroussé nose, which serve her well before the camera. And guided by Mr. Santell she is most competent in a part that demands a great deal."

"I was told I had given an Academy Award performance, in retrospect," said Miss O'Day. The Academy of Motion Picture Arts and

Sciences was established in 1927. In addition, she was selected as a Wampas Baby Star in 1928. Her sister Sally had been chosen for this honor in 1926. "Naturally if you do something that is very good you get other offers."

One of those offers was to work with her sister in *The Lovelorn* (1927). She later would appear with her in the appropriately titled *Sisters* (1930) and both are briefly featured together in *Show of Shows* (1929).

The Lovelorn (1927, MGM). Molly O'Day and sister Sally O'Neil (kneeling).

The Lovelorn (1927, MGM) with Molly O'Day and Larry Kent.

"The family was very close and it was a delight to work with them. My sister was my favorite [actress] to work with. It was enjoyable just to be her sister and just to *have* her for a sister."

MOTHER GOT ALL MY CHECKS

Those roaring twenties would soon lead way into the era of the talking film. Molly talked about some of the changes and what it meant to be a screen star at the time when silent films reigned but talkies would soon be in vogue.

"Well you had to be usually on the set and ready to go very, very early, six-thirty or seven A.M. so that gives you an idea of what time we'd start. On different days there were different times according to what they [the studio] had scheduled for that day and how long it would take to accomplish it.

"Everything we did on a 'promotional' basis for a film or a studio was always a 'big splash.' They always had music on the set and you could be talked to [from the sidelines] while filming. I was under eighteen so mother got all my checks and you paid no taxes.

"Naturally, talkies. We were never tested for our voices. I imagine it was obvious that we would be fine. You either spoke well or you didn't.

The Noonan Sisters: Molly O'Day (L) and Sally O'Neil, July 1927.

You either had a nice speaking voice or you didn't. I did not have that problem. Most people that I knew could speak; they all had good voices."

Molly worked for several studios at one time or another but admitted she didn't really have a favorite one. "It was the *people* you worked with that became favorites, not the studio." She acknowledged also that once a player was under contract with a certain studio, one did as told. "That was entirely up to them. I did okay. I didn't *dislike* being under a contract."

THE WEIGHT ISSUE

A somewhat dismal and painful time for Molly occurred during the course of 1928–29. She had gained weight, most probably due to her adolescence and nothing to do with eating too much. Regardless, the studio told Molly to shed the pounds or face the consequences. One must remember the 1920s were the age of the flapper, when stick figured, bosomless girls were in style. After all, those beads had to hang straight down the front of a young lady's dress!

It seems ridiculous in retrospect to have ever considered Molly obese, especially when one considers some of our current cinema "icons." Nonetheless, it did cost her an important role, which went instead to Dorothy MacKail. The film was *The Barker* (1928).

The weight issue infuriated many of Molly's fans. One in particular, Lucille Boyd from Tacoma, Washington, made her feelings known. In an editorial to one of the popular movie magazines in 1928, she wrote the following: "I see Molly O'Day is not allowed to be a star because she has put on a few pounds of weight. If directors chose stars that had a few curves instead of girls that look like sticks, I would be better pleased. When you go to a show nowadays, all you see are girls who look like a bag of bones."

I had asked Molly's daughter Virginia if the stories were true. She told me yes, and that only until very recently had Molly shared this with her daughter. When asked to reflect on that time in her life, Molly stated simply that "it bothered and saddened me."

She left the film industry in 1935, but not after encompassing a stint in vaudeville and maintaining an active film career. Molly would marry the popular comedian Jack Durant, whose extreme good looks and handsome physique were said to have resembled that of Clark Gable. The Durant's had three daughters and one son.

I asked Molly how she'd like to be remembered, what she felt was her greatest contribution. She laughed. "My greatest contribution? I will leave that up to someone else to say. I was happy to be an actress. I was a 'natural,' and because of it, I remain, remembered. I was a good actress and that was it."

FILMOGRAPHY

The Patent Leather Kid—1927. First National Pictures. Silent. B&W. 35mm. 12 reels, 11,955 feet. *Presented by:* Richard A. Rowland. *Producer/Director:* Alfred Santell. *Scenario:* Winifred Dunn. *Title:* Gerald C. Duffy. *Adaptation:* Adela Rogers St. Johns. *Photography:* Arthur Edeson, Ralph Hammeras, Alvin Knechtel. *Production Manager:* Al Rockett. *Makeup:* Fred C. Ryle. *Cast:* Richard Barthelmess, Molly O'Day, Lawford Davidson, Matthew Betz, Arthur Stone, Raymond Turner, Hank Mann, Walter James, Lucien Prival, Nigel DeBrulier, Fred O'Beck, Cliff Salam, Henry Murdock, Charles Sullivan, John Kolb, Al Albron.

The Lovelorn—1927. Cosmopolitan Productions. *Distributor:* Metro-Goldwyn-Mayer Distributing Corp. Silent. B&W. 35mm. 7 reels, 6,110 feet. *Director:* John P. McCarthy. *Scenario:* Bradley King. *Title:* Frederic Hatton. *Story:* Beatric Fairfax. *Photography:* Henry Sharp. *Set Design:* Cedric Gibbons, Alexander Toluboff. *Film Editors:* John W. English, Gilbert Clark. *Cast:* Sally O'Neil, Molly O'Day, Larry Kent, James Murray, Charles Delaney, George Cooper, Allan Forrest, Dorothy Cumming.

Hard-Boiled Haggerty—1927. First National Pictures. Silent. B&W. 35mm. 8 reels, 7,443 feet. *Presented by:* Richard A. Rowland. *Producer:* Wid Gunning. *Director:* Charles Brabin. *Scenario:* Carey Wilson. *Photography:* Sol Polito. *Costumes:* Walter Plunkett. *Cast:* Milton Sills, Molly O'Day, Mitchell Lewis, Arthur Stone, George Fawcett, Yola D'Avril.

The Shepherd of the Hills—1928. First National Pictures. Silent. B&W. 35mm. 9 reels, 8,188 feet. *Presented by:* Richard A. Rowland. *Producer:* Charles R. Rogers. *Director:* Albert Rogell. *Adaptation/Continuity:* Marion Jackson. *Title:* Dwinelle Benthall, Rufus McCosh. *Photography:* Sol Polito. *Film Editor:* Hugh Bennett. *Cast:* Alec B. Francis, Molly O'Day, John Boles, Matthew Betz, Romaine Fielding, Otis Harlan, Joseph Bennett, Maurice Murphy, Edythe Chapman, Carl Stockdale, Marian Douglas, John Westwood.

The Little Shepherd of Kingdom Come—1928. First National Pictures. Silent. B&W. 35mm. 8 reels, 7,700 feet. *Presented by:* Richard A. Rowland. *Supervisor:* Henry Hobert. *Producer/Director:* Alfred Santell. *Scenario:* Bess Meredyth. *Title:* Dwinelle Benthall, Rufus McCosh. *Camera:* Lee Garmes. *Film Editor:* Hugh Bennett. *Cast:* Richard Barthelmess, Molly O'Day, Nelson McDowell, Martha Mattox, Victor Potel, Mark Hamilton, William Bertram, Walter Lewis, Gardner James, Ralph Yearsley, Gustav von Seyffertitz, Robert Milasch, Claude Gillingwater, David Torrence, Eulalie Jensen, Doris Dawson, Walter Rogers.

Sea Devils—1931. Larry Darmour Productions. Standard Pictures Corp. *Distributor:* Continental Talking Pictures Corp. Sound (RCA Photophone Recording). B&W. 6 reels. 58 or 60 min. Passed by the National Board of Review. *Presented by:* W. Ray Johnston. *Director:* Joseph Levering. *Assistant Director:* Paul Malvern. *Writer:* Scott Littleton. *Photography:* James Brown. *Sets:* Frank Dexter. *Editor:* Dwight Caldwell. *Sound Engineers:* Neil Jack and Charles Franklin. *Cast:* Molly O'Day, Edmund Burns, Walter Long, Paul Panzer, Henry Otto, Ted Storback, William Moran, [James Daonneylly], [Jules Cowles].

Sob Sister—1931. Fox Film Corp. Alfred Santell Production. *Distributor:* Fox Film Corp. Sound (Western Electric System). B&W. 7 feels, 6,400 feet. 71 min. Passed by the National Board of Review. *Director:* Alfred Santell. *Assistant Director:* Marty Santell. *Scenario:* Edwin Burke. *Contributing Writ-*

ers: Bradley King and Maurine Watkins. *Photography:* Glenn MacWilliams. *Second Camera:* Joseph MacDonald and Blakeley Wagner. *Assistant Camera:* L.B. Abbott and Frank McDonald. *Art Director:* Robert Haas. *Film Editor:* Ralph Dietrich. *Sound Recording:* George Leverett. *Still Photography:* Charles Schoenbaum. *Cast:* James Dunn, Linda Watkins, Minna Gombell, Howard Phillips, George E. Stone, Molly O'Day, Eddie Dillon, George Byron, Lex Lindsay, Harold Waldridge, Neal Burns, Ernest Wood, Harry Beresford, Sarah Padden, Charles Middleton, Joe Brown, George Chandler, Edwin Sturgis, Maurice Black, Clifford Dempsey, Wally Albright, Ward Bond, [Edwin Burke].

The Devil on Deck—1932. Sono Art/World Wide Pictures, Inc. *Distributor:* Sono Art/World Wide Pictures, Inc. Sound. B&W. 6 reels. *Presented by:* George W. Weeks. *Director:* Wallace W. Fox. *Scenario:* Bernard McConville. *Cast:* Reed Howes, Molly O'Day, Wheeler Oakman, June Marlowe, Kenneth Treseder, Rolfe Sedan, A.S. Byron, Constantine Romanoff.

Gigolettes of Paris—1933. Equitable Pictures, Inc. Controlled by Majestic Pictures Corp. *Distributor:* Equitable Pictures, Inc. Sound (RCA Photophone Recording). B&W. 6 reels. 59, 61 or 64 min. Passed by the National Board of Review. *Director:* Alphonse Martell. *Story:* Alphonse Martell. *Additional Dialogue:* Mary Flannery. *Photography:* Henry Cronjager and Herman Schopp. *Art*

Director: Mack D'Agostino. *Sets:* Tec-Art Studios, Inc. *Film Editors:* Thomas Persons and [Otis Garrett]. *Sound Recording:* L.E. Tope. *Production Manager:* J.E. Petral. *Cast:* Madge Bellamy, Gilbert Roland, Natalie Moorhead, Theodore von Eltz, Molly O'Day, Henry Kolker, Paul Porcassi, Albert Conti, F. Schumann-Heink, Maude Truax, Lester New, Robert Bolder.

The Life of Vergie Winters—1934. RKO Pictures, Inc. A Pandro S. Berman Production. *Distributor:* RKO Radio Pictures, Inc. Sound (RCA Victor System). B&W. 9 reels. 73 or 82–83 min. Passed by the National Board of Review. *Director:* Alfred Santell. *Scenario:* Jane Murfin. *Photography:* Lucien Andriot. *Camera:* Pierre Moles. *Assistant Camera:* Kay Norton. *Art Directors:* Van Nest Polglase and Charles Kirk. *Editor:* George Hively. *Costumes:* Walter Plunkett. *Music:* Max Steiner. *Recording:* D.A. Cutler. *Music Re-recording:* Murray Spivack. *Still Photography:* John Miehle. *Cast:* Ann Harding, John Boles, Helen Vinson, Betty Furness, Frank Albertson, Creighton Chaney, Sara Haden, Molly O'Day, Ben Alexander, Donald Crisp, Maidel Turner, Cecil Cunningham, Wesley Berry, Edward Van Sloan, Josephine Whittell, Wallis Clark, Edwin Stanley, Dorothy Sebastian, Walter Brennan, Bonita Granville, Edwin Maxwell.

Hired Wife—1934. Pinnacle Productions, Inc. *Distributor:* State Rights. Pinnacle Productions, Inc. Sound. B&W. 60 or 65 min. *Pre-sented by:* J.D. Trop. *Director:* George Melford. *Scenario:* Alma Sioux Scarberry. *Photography:* Mark Stengler. *Art Directors:* Robert Stevens and Frank Drdlik. *Film Editor:* Helene Turner. *Music score:* George Henninger. *Recording Engineer:* Percy Glenn and T.C. Parker III. *Cast:* Greta Nissen, Weldon Heyburn, James Kirkwood, Molly O'Day, Jane Winton, Blanche Taylor, Carolyn Gates, Evelyn Bennett.

Skull and Crown—1935. Reliable Pictures Corp. *Distributor:* State Rights. Reliable Pictures Corp. Sound. B&W. 58–59 min. Passed by the National Board of Review. *Presented by:* Bernard B. Ray. *Associate Producer:* Harry S. Webb. *Director:* Elmer Clifton. *Assistant Director:* Bernard Deroux. *Story:* James Oliver Curwood. *Dialogue:* Ben Cohen. *Continuity:* Carl Krusada. *Photography:* Pliny Goodfriend. *Art Director:* Ira Webb. *Editor:* Fred Bain. *Sound:* Jesse Moulin. *Cast:* Rin-Tin-Tin, Jr., Regis Toomey, Jack Mulhall, Molly O'Day, Jack Mower, Lois January, James Murry, John Elliott, Tom London, Milburn Moranti, Robert Walker.

Lawless Border—1935. Spectrum Pictures Corp. *Distributors:* State Rights, Spectrum Pictures Corp. Sound. B&W. 58 min. *Producer:* Ray Kirkwood. *Director:* J.P. McCarthy. *Author:* Zara Tazil. *Camera:* Robert Cline. *Cast:* Bill Cody, Molly O'Day, Martin Garralaga, Ted Adams, Joe De La Cruz, John Elliot, Merrill McCormick.

Anita Page

My phone rang one evening and Miss Page's assistant and long-time friend, film star Randal Malone, told me that she had agreed to a "by mail" interview. Randal asked me to submit no more than ten questions to her for review. I was delighted as I had tried to attain *any* type of interview with Miss Page for some time. "She's one of the [last] great silent stars left," he quipped. I knew this, of course, and wasted no time in sending her off my list of questions, carefully thought out.

Then, almost one year later, I was able to do a short telephone interview with Miss Page as well as the written one. She was indeed delightful, and her voice and memory certainly did *not* give any indication I was speaking to a woman in her nineties.

I received the interview back from her secretary, Carol, who, like Randal, was also instrumental in arranging this endeavor. What follows are Miss Page's remembrances of her career—those she worked with, the stars, directors, early Hollywood and her comparison to "talkies." I hope the reader not only finds enjoyment here, but also a deeper understanding of what it was like then to work in cinema at a time when change was happening almost daily in the film world.

HOLLYWOOD: 1920S STYLE

I was most anxious for Miss Page, as well as the other players represented in this book, to tell me about early Hollywood and those pioneering years. "I would say that the 1920s Hollywood, as well as the thirties Hollywood was an exciting time of celebrities and many social

A ravishing Anita Page in 1928.

functions that a film star was expected to attend. It was part of your job to go and be seen in all the glamorous night spots.

"However, work was work and that was the most important part of your career. As 5:00 A.M. came very early, I would set a time limit as to when I had to be back in bed and I kept to it! Now on the nights when I didn't have to be at the studio so early or I was off that day, I would stay out and enjoy all the wonderful music and lovely people and places."

Anita Page was chosen as one of the Wampas Baby Stars of 1929. Many young starlets received this honor, which was a vote of confidence from the industry that you were considered an up and coming star. (Molly O'Day was selected in 1927 and her sister Sally O'Neil in 1926.)

"It was certainly an honor! Being a silent film star in 1929 meant you were going to be in for some changes because of the coming of sound to the movies. So at that time in Hollywood, I felt it important [to be] chosen as a Wampas Baby Star. It meant that you could be hopeful about your future in pictures."

Our Dancing Daughters, 1928: Anita on the arm of Johnny Mack Brown.

Not all stars who received this "stamp" of approval made the crossover successfully to talkies. What, I wondered, was it like for players at this time? The fear of the microphone proved a cruel reality for some.

"It was a time of *tragedy and triumph.* The tragic part for so many of my contemporaries was that because of their voices, not being suited for sound pictures, they were out of a job. Even though some of the stars had achieved great success in silent films and were even idolized by the public, still their careers were over.

"This was very sad. For some, it meant their whole life was over. The triumph part was that sound opened the door for musicals! Almost overnight, actors came or were brought to the studio from New York because of their stage or musical talents.

"It was 1928, and that was when I was given the news that I was about to be starred in MGM's very first "All Talking! All Singing! All Dancing!" musical: *The Broadway Melody*! I was simply overwhelmed. Not only because I was a silent movie star making the big crossover into the talkies, but because the studio had selected me for what they hoped was going to be the biggest picture of the year! And guess what, it was!

"*The Broadway Melody* broke box office records and [it] won the Academy Award for the "best picture" of 1929! Not bad huh?"

RAMON NOVARRO

"I was so very blessed to have worked with so many of the greats of our business—Lon Chaney, [Buster] Keaton, [John] Gilbert, [Clark] Gable, just to name a few. However, one of my very special memories, (and I do have so very many wonderful memories) would be Ramon Novarro. When we were working together he had a way of making it all so much fun. As I loved the work anyway, he would go out of his way to put you at ease and we'd end up having a wonderful time every day.

"Ramon and I became so close during that period. In fact, I was the only gal he ever asked to marry [him] that I knew of. Of course, I said no, I just didn't think it would work. But I must say how fond I was of him, and treasure our friendship to this day."

In reality, it was common knowledge within the movie crowd that Mr. Novarro preferred the sexual company of men. Anita politely referred to his preference as "his circumstance."

"When he asked me to marry I told him, 'Oh, maybe on an off Thursday," she laughed. "Actually I couldn't marry anyone who took longer to get ready than *I* did! If all my leading men had been like Ramon, I could have relaxed!"

Years later Ramon Novarro was bludgeoned to death when a couple of hoodlums broke into his residence. Anita Page was one of the first to get a call from his family and she recalled that horrible day and the loss of one of her very favorite people.

"Ramon's brother called me and said, 'I want to tell you Anita before you see the paper,'

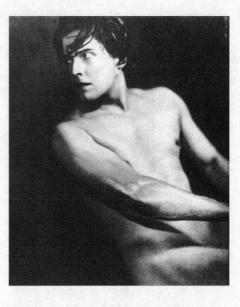

Ramon Novarro as Ben-Hur, the Galley Slave (photo by Brogaglio, 1926 Rome).

so it would kind of absorb the shock. They called me immediately when he was dead. I couldn't believe it. I felt so terrible. He had always been very wonderful to me. This marvelous poor man that did so much for people and then this terrible thing [with] these men hurting him. I don't even want to think about that. Ramon was my *favorite* leading man and Randal—Randal Malone."

L.B. MAYER: STAR MAKER

"I had a great deal of respect for Mr. Mayer [Louis B. Mayer, studio head at Metro-Goldwyn-Mayer Studios]. I must say I admired his manner, the way he groomed each star (if he liked you and you remained in his favor). His power was tremendous!

"He had the means to make an actor a great star and he made many great stars. What he did for me during my early days at Metro was wonderful. I had great parts, in great pictures. After awhile, he asked certain things of me that I would not do. I don't have any regrets about that as he kept me at the studio under contract my entire seven years. I stood my ground with him, and in the end [I] was better for it."

Anita Page, the epitome of glamour, circa 1930.

Mayer had an affinity for beautiful women and Anita Page was no exception. When he tried to get her in bed, however, that's when Anita drew the line.

"He told me, 'I can make you the biggest star in the world in three pictures' and he snapped his fingers like that. 'I could also kill Garbo in three pictures, and he snapped his fingers. But I said, 'Mr. Mayer, I am *already* a star.' He said, 'I could make you *bigger*, we could handle things discreetly' but I told him I didn't play that way.

"There was one time when we were on location and Mr. and Mrs. Mayer were visiting on the set. Mr. Mayer said to his wife, 'It's getting dark and I'm alone here with Anita.' And Mrs. Mayer said, 'Oh don't worry, I *trust* Anita!

"He didn't say too many more things to me after that. I was very fond of Mrs. Mayer. I was very happy to be working with him but I would not play any games. He wanted to play romantic games and I simply was *not going to*! I liked him as a boss but that's where it ended."

MASTERS OF THEIR ART

"Lon Chaney was a masterful artist. When we were working together, he taught me so very much about the art of screen acting. I remember he would say, 'Use your eyes to express emotions.' He worked very hard at creating characters for the screen and through him, I learned

(L to R) Bessie Love, Charles King, and Anita Page in *The Broadway Melody* (1929, MGM) (courtesy of Anita Page).

the importance of facial expression and body movement to achieve a particular intention for a scene. Again, these were *silent* pictures.

"I wasn't in Hollywood during the Arbuckle tragedy so I can't say much about it. Of course, the loss of Rudy Valentino was one of the great tragedies of that era. Partly because he was so young; that's always sad. But also because of what he meant to so *many*. He, like so many of our early movie idols, could *not* be replaced. He was an original in a period of history when we were all creating something for the first time. Now they call it the 'Golden Era.' How *marvelous* for me to have been a part of that!

"I would have to say that Joan [Crawford] had more ambition than most actresses I worked with. We made three pictures together, four if you count *Hollywood Review*. I found her to be a very hard worker, always professional and dedicated to being a star. In those days we knew how to be a *star*.

"During my career as a film star of 'Hollywood's Golden Era,' I had occasions where Pola [Negri] and I met. I remember she was very much the grand screen actress, even in person, and why not? After all, it was rather expected of most of us.

"I never worked with her in any films; however, my close friend and ex-husband, Nacio Herb Brown, a great songwriter for MGM, knew her [and] worked with her on some music for one of her pictures. He arranged for Pola and I to meet and have lunch a couple of times. She was fascinating! She loved being a movie star and so did I.

"Her reputation, much like her screen image, was one of glamour. She played it to the hilt. I admired that, also I found her to be nice, I liked that too."

LOVE FOR THE SILENT FILMS

"Without any question, I loved making silent films more than the talkies! You see, acting in silent pictures was so very wonderful for me. It was a different style of acting then. You were more free to express emotion through your *face*, moreover, your *eyes*! Also, without sound, they [studio musicians] would play beautiful mood music for me while I was acting. This would help inspire me, really set the pace for the scene.

"The klieg lights were very bright but I grew accustomed to their extreme brightness. Maybe because the bright lights in my eyes could not compete with the stars I also had in them! It was all so beautiful then.

"I loved the silent films most of all": a striking Anita Page.

"The saddest part for me when the silent film era ended was the fact that my style of acting had to change. Acting in silents was a great [deal] of fun for me. It was a style all its own, bigger than life! I missed it terribly.

"In talkies, you had to concentrate on where the microphone was and be very careful not to upset it or make any kind or movement or sound that might be heard.

"If you did, that meant taking the scene all over again. Talkies took some getting use to for me and I must say, I was delighted with my success in sound pictures. But I loved the silent films most of all!

"As a rule, I didn't go to see my own movies unless it was required for me to appear. What I mean by required is simply this: sometimes the studio would ask me to appear at an opening of one of my films or tour the big cities and make special personal appearances along with the film itself.

"I remember touring with *Our Dancing Daughters* [1928], and as I remember that was the first time I sat and watched myself on screen. Much to my surprise, I *loved* it! *It was marvelous!*"

The First Academy Awards

The Academy of Motion Picture Arts and Sciences was founded in Hollywood in 1927.

Anita Page was there to see Janet Gaynor accept her award for best actress as well as Emil Jannings for best actor. I asked her to please talk about this "first" in Hollywood history.

"I went to the first Academy Awards Ceremony at the Hotel Roosevelt in Hollywood. I remember it was held in the

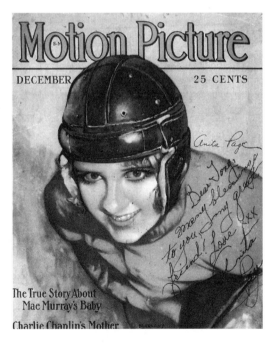

Anita Page plays football (!) on the cover of *Motion Picture* magazine, December 1928.

Orange Blossom Room and was so very beautiful. All the stars were there!

"I remember seeing most of my studio pals, like Marion Davies, Ramon Navarro and Buster Keaton to name a few. I recall they served dinner in those days and the entire evening was just marvelous!

"The next year, the Academy Awards were held at the Ambassador Hotel. That's the year *The Broadway Melody* [1929] won best picture. I was thrilled. As the star of the film, I felt very pleased with myself. It was all so wonderful."

I asked Miss Page about her favorite memories and what, if any, philosophy she embraced regarding her work. After all, it is indeed rare to see a star of the twenties still before the camera in the nineties. Page filmed *Hollywood Mortuary* (1998) and *Sunset After Dark* (1996) with MTV star, Randal Malone.

"Love your work! Darling I have so many favorite memories of my career, but at my age I'm afraid there is not enough time to share them all with you. I will say this, I *loved* being a movie star! It was *marvelous!*"

FILMOGRAPHY

Telling the World—1928. Metro-Goldwyn-Mayer Pictures. Silent. B&W. 35mm. 8 reels. 7,184 feet. *Director:* Sam Wood. *Scenario:* Raymond L. Schrock. *Title:* Joe Farnham. *Story:* Dale Van Every. *Photography:* William Daniels. *Sets:* Cedric Gibbons. *Film Editors:* Margaret Booth, John Colton. *Wardrobe:* Gilbert Clark. *Cast:* William Haines, Anita Page, Eileen Percy, Frank Currier, Polly Moran, Bert Roach, William V. Mong, Matthew Betz.

While the City Sleeps—1928. Metro-Goldwyn-Mayer Pictures. Sound effects and Music Score (Movietone). B&W. 35mm. 9 reels. 7,231 feet. *Director:* Jack Henry Sharp. *Sets:* Cedric Gib-bons. *Film Editor:* Sam S. Zimbal-ist. *Wardrobe:* Gilbert Clark. *Cast:* Lon Chaney, Anita Page, Carroll Nye, Wheeler Oakman, Mae Busch, Polly Moran, Lydia Yea-mans Titus, William Orlamond, Richard Carle.

Our Dancing Daughters—1928. Cosmopolitan Productions. *Distributor:* Metro-Goldwyn-Mayer Distributing Corp. Sound Effects and Music Score (Movietone). B&W. 35mm. 9 reels. 7,652 feet. *Director:* Harry Beaumont. *Story/ Continuity:* Josephine Lovett. *Title:* Marian Ainslee, Ruth Cummings. *Photography:* George Barnes. *Sets:* Cedric Gibbons. *Film Editor:* William Hamilton. *Cast:* Joan Crawford, John Mack Brown, Nils

Asther, Dorothy Sebastian, Anita Page, Kathlyn Williams, Edward Nugent, Dorothy Cumming, Huntly Gordon, Evelyn Hall, Sam De Grasse.

Navy Blues—1929. Metro-Goldwyn-Mayer Pictures. Sound (Movietone). B&W. 35mm. 9 reels. 6,936 feet. *Director:* Clarence Brown, Dial J.C. Nugent, Elliott Nugent, W.L. River. *Adaptation:* Dale Van Every. *Story:* Raymond L. Schrock. *Photography:* Merritt B. Gerstad. *Art Director:* Cedric Gibbons. *Film Editor:* Hugh Wynn. *Cast:* William Haines, Anita Page, Karl Dane, J.C. Nugent, Edythe Chapman, Gertrude Sutton, Wade Boteler.

The Hollywood Revue of 1929—Metro-Goldwyn-Mayer Pictures. Sound (Movietone). B&W with color sequences (Technicolor). 35mm. 13 reels. 11,669 feet. *Producer:* Harry RapF. *Director:* Charles Reisner. *Dialogue:* Al Boasberg, Robert E. Hopkins. *Skit by:* Joe Farnham. *Photography:* John Arnold, Irving Ries, Maximilian Fabian, John M. Nickolaus. *Art Directors:* Cedric Gibbons, Richard Day. *Film Editors:* William S. Gray, Cameron K. Wood. *Cast:* Conrad Nagel, Jack Benny, John Gilbert, Norma Shearer, Joan Crawford, Bessie Love, Lionel Barrymore, Cliff Edwards, Stan Laurel, Oliver Hardy, Anita Page, Nils Asther, The Brox Sisters, Natacha Natova and Co., Marion Davies, William Haines, Buster Keaton, Marie Dressler, Charles King, Polly Moran, Gus Edwards, Karl Dane, George K. Arthur, Ann Dvorak, Gwen Lee, Albertina Rasch Ballet,

The Rounders, The Biltmore Quartet.

The Broadway Melody—1929. Metro-Goldwyn-Mayer Pictures. Los Angeles premier. Sound (Movietone). B&W with color sequences (Technicolor). 35mm. 10 reels. 9,372 feet. (Also silent 5,943 feet.) *Director:* Harry Beaumont. *Ensemble numbers staged by:* George Cunningham. *Scenario:* Sarah Y. Mason. *Dialogue:* Norman Houston, James Gleason. *Title:* Earl Baldwin. *Story:* Edmund Goulding. *Photography:* John Arnold. *Art Director:* Cedric Gibbons. *Film Editor:* Sam S. Zimbalist. *Cast:* Anita Page, Bessie Love, Charles King, Jed Prouty, Kenneth Thomson, Edward Dillon, Mary Doran, Eddie Kane, J. Emmett Bect, Marshall Ruth, Drew Demarest.

The Flying Fleet—1929. Metro-Goldwyn-Mayer Pictures. Synchronized music score. B&W. 35mm. 11 reels 9,044 feet. (Also silent.) *Director:* George Hill. *Screenplay:* Richard Schayer. *Title:* Joe Farnham. *Story:* Lieutenant Commander Frank Wead, U.S.N. *Photography:* Ira Morgan. *Air Photography:* Charles A. Marshall. *Art Director:* Cedric Gibbons. *Film Editor:* Blanche Sewell. *Cast:* Ramon Novarro, Ralph Graves, Anita Page, Edward Nugent, Carroll Nye, Sumner Getchell, Gardner James, Alfred Allen, The Three Sea Hawks.

Speedway—1929. Metro-Goldwyn-Mayer Pictures. Music Score and Sound Effects (Movietone). B&W. 35mm. 8 reels. 6,962 or 7,075 feet. (Also silent.) *Director:* Harry Beaumont. *Title:* Joe Farnham.

Adaptation: Alfred Block, Ann Price, Byron Morgan. *Story:* Byron Morgan. *Photography:* Henry Sharp. *Art Director:* Cedric Gibbons. *Film Editor:* George Hively. *Wardrobe:* David Cox. *With the cooperation of:* Indianapolis Speedway Association. *Cast:* William Haines, Anita Page, Ernest Torrence, Karl Dane, John Miljan, Eugenie Besserer, Polly Moran.

War Nurse—1930. Metro-Goldwyn-Mayer Pictures. Sound (Movietone). B&W. 35mm. 9 reels, 7,333 feet. *Director:* Edgar Selwyn. *Scenario:* Becky Gardiner. *Additional Dialogue:* Joe Farnham. *Photography:* Charles Rosher. *Art Director:* Cedric Gibbons. *Film Editor:* William Le Vanway. *Recording Engineer:* Douglas Shearer. *Wardrobe:* René Hubert. *Cast:* Robert Montgomery, Anita Page, June Walerk, Robert Ames, ZaSu Pitts, Marie Prevost, Helen Jerome Eddy, Hedda Hopper, Edward Nugent, Martha Sleeper, Michael Vavitch.

Gentleman's Fate—1931. Metro-Goldwyn-Mayer Corp. Controlled by Loew's, Inc. *Distributor:* Metro-Goldwyn-Mayer Distributing Corp. Sound (Western Electric Sound System). B&W. 10 reels. 90 or 93 min. Passed by the National Board of Review. *Supervisor:* Harry Rapf. *Director:* Mervyn LeRoy. *Dialogue Continuity:* Leonard Praskins. *Photography:* Merritt B. Gerstad. *Art Director:* Cedric Gibbons. *Film Editor:* William S. Gray. *Wardrobe:* René Hubert. *Recording Director:* Douglas Shearer. *Cast:* John Gilbert, Louis Wolheim, Leila Hyams, Anita Page, Marie Prevost, John Miljan,

George Cooper, Ferike Boros, Ralph Ince, Frank Reicher, Paul Porcasi, Tenen Holtz.

The Easiest Way—1931. Metro-Goldwyn-Mayer Corp. Controlled by Loew's, Inc. *Distributor:* Metro-Goldwyn-Mayer Distributing Corp. Sound (Western Electric Sound System). B&W. 8 reels. 73 min. Passed by the National Board of Review. *Producer:* Hunt Stromberg. *Director:* Jack Conway. *Assistant Director:* Al Shenberg and Red Golden. *Adaptation:* Edith Ellis. *Photography:* John Mescall. *Art Director:* Cedric Gibbons. *Film Editor:* Frank Sullivan. *Gowns:* René Hubert. *Recording Director:* Douglas Shearer. *Cast:* Constance Bennett, Adolphe Menjou, Robert Montgomery, Marjorie Rambeau, Anita Page, J. Farrell MacDonald, Clara Blandick, Clark Gable, Hedda Hopper, Charles Judels, John Harron, Dell Henderson, Elizabeth Ann Keever, Andy Shuford, Jack Hanlon.

Reducing—1931. Metro-Goldwyn-Mayer Corp. Controlled by Loew's, Inc. *Distributor:* Metro-Goldwyn-Mayer Corp. Sound (Western Electric Sound System). B&W. 8 reels. 75 or 77 min. Passed by the National Board of Review. *Director:* Charles F. Riesner. *Assistant Director:* Sandy Roth. *Dialogue Continuity:* Willard Mack and Beatric Banyard. *Additional Dialogue:* Robert E. Hopkins and Zelda Sears. *Photography:* Leonard Smith. *Art Director:* Cedric Gibbons. *Film Editor:* William Le Vanway. *Wardrobe:* René Hubert. *Recording Director:* Douglas Shearer. *Cast:* Marie Dressler, Polly Moran, Anita Page, Lucien

Littlefield, Buster Collier, Jr., Sally Eilers, William Bakewell, Billy Naylor, Jay Ward.

Sidewalks of New York—1931. Metro-Goldwyn-Mayer Corp. Controlled by Loew's Inc. A Buster Keaton Production. *Distributor:* Metro-Goldwyn-Mayer Distributing Corp. Sound (Western Electric Sound System). B&W. 8 reels. 70–71 min. Passed by the National Board of Review. *Directors:* Jules White and Zion Myers. *Assistant Director:* Bob Barnes. *Story:* George Landry and Paul Gerard Smith. *Dialogue:* Robert E. Hopkins, Eric Hatch and Willard Mack. *Photography:* Leonard Smith. *Art Director:* Cedric Gibbons. *Film Editors:* Charles Hochberg and Basil Wrangell. *Recording Director:* Douglas Shearer. *Cast:* Buster Keaton, Anita Page, Cliff Edwards, Frank Rowan, Norman Phillips, Jr., Frank LaRue, Oscar Apfel, Syd Saylor, Clark Marshall.

Under 18—1932. Warner Bros. Pictures, Inc. *Distributor:* Warner Bros. Pictures, Inc. The Vitaphone Corp. Warner Bros. Pictures, Inc. Sound. B&W. 9 reels. 79–81 min. *Director:* Archie Mayo. *Script:* Charles Kenyon and Maude Fulton. *Dialogue:* Charles Kenyon. *Photography:* Barney McGill. *Art Director:* Esdras Hartley. *Editor:* George Marks. *Gowns:* Earl Luick. *Vitaphone Orchestra conductor:* Leo F. Forbstein. *Cast:* Marian Mash, Anita Page, Regis Toomey, Warren William, Norman Foster, Joyce Compton, J. Farrell MacDonald, Claire Dodd, Paul Porcasi, Maude Eburne, Murray Kinnell, Dorothy Appleby, Judith Vosselli, Mary Doran, Walter McGrail, Emma Dunn.

Are You Listening?—1932. Metro-Goldwyn-Mayer. Controlled by Metro-Goldwyn-Mayer Distributing Corp. *Distributor:* Metro-Goldwyn-Mayer Distributing Corp. Sound (Western Electric Sound System). B&W. 8 reels. 73 or 76 min. Passed by the National Board of Review. *Director:* Harry Beaumont. *Assistant Director:* Harry Bucquet. *Adaptation:* Dwight Taylor. *Photography:* Harold Rosson. *Art Director:* Cedric Gibbons. *Film Editor:* Frank Sullivan. *Recording Director:* Douglas Shearer. *Cast:* William Haines, Madge Evans, Anita Page, Karen Morley, Neil Hamilton, Wallace Ford, Jean Hersholt, Joan Marsh, John Miljan, Murray Kinnell, Ethel Griffies, Hattie McDaniel, Rolfe Sedan, Louise Carter, Charles Coleman, Charley Grapewin, Frank Whitbeck, Herman Bing.

Skyscraper Souls—1932. Metro-Goldwyn-Mayer. Controlled by Loew's Inc., a Cosmopolitan Production. *Distributor:* Metro-Goldwyn-Mayer Distributing Corp. Sound (Western Electric Sound System). B&W. 10 reels. 80 or 99 min. Passed by the National Board of Review. *Director:* Edgar Selwyn. *Assistant Director:* Cullen Tate. *Dialogue Continuity:* Elmer Harris. *Adaptation:* C. Gardner Sullivan. *Photography:* William Daniels. *Art Director:* Cedric Gibbons. *Film Editor:* Tom Held. *Recording Director:* Douglas Shearer. *Sound:* Fred Morgan. *Cast:* Warren William, Maureen O'Sullivan, Gregory Ratoff, Anita Page,

Verree Teasdale, Norman Foster, George Barbier, Jean Hersholt, Wallace Ford, Hedda Hopper, Helen Coburn, John Marston, Purnell B. Pratt, Arnold Lucy, Edward Brophy, Billy Gilbert, Tom Kennedy.

Night Court—1932. Metro-Goldwyn-Mayer. Controlled by Loew's Inc. *Distributor:* Metro-Goldwyn-Mayer Distributing Corp. Sound (Western Electric Sound System). B&W. 9 reels. 89 or 95 min. Passed by the National Board of Review. *Director:* W.S. Van Dyke. *Assistant Director:* Jay Marchant. *Script:* Bayard Veiller and Lenore Coffee. *Photography:* Norbert Broding. *Art Director:* Cedric Gibbons. *Film Editor:* Ben Lewis. *Recording Director:* Douglas Shearer. *Sound:* Ralph Shugart. *Cast:* Phillips Holmes, Walter Huston, Anita Page, Lewis Stone, Mary Carlisle, John Miljan, Jean Hersholt, Rafaela Ottiano, Eily Malyon.

Prosperity—1932. Metro-Goldwyn-Mayer. Controlled by Loew's Inc., a Sam Wood Production. *Distributor:* Metro-Goldwyn-Mayer Distributing Corp. Sound (Western Electric Sound System). B&W. 9 reels. 76 or 87 min. Passed by the National Board of Review. *Director:* Sam Wood. *Script:* Zelda Sears and Eve Greene. *Story:* Sylvia Thalberg and Frank Butler. *Photography:* Leonard Smith. *Art Director:* Cedric Gibbons. *Film Editor:* William LeVanway. *Recording Director:* Douglas Shearer. *Sound:* Fred Morgan. *Cast:* Marie Dressler, Polly Moran, Anita Page, Norman Foster, John Miljan, Jacquie Lynn, Jerry Tucker, Charles Giblyn, Frank

Darien, Henry Armetta, John Roche, Edward Brophy, Billy Gilbert.

Soldiers of the Storm—1933. Columbia Pictures Corp. *Distributor:* Columbia Pictures Corp. Sound. B&W. 7 reels. 67–68 min. *Director:* D. Ross Lederman. *Assistant Director:* Wilbur McGaugh. *Script:* Charles Condon. *Story:* Thomson Burtis. *Dialogue:* Horace McCoy. *Photography:* Teddy Tetzlaff. *Film Editor:* Maurice Wright. *Sound Engineer:* George Cooper. *Cast:* Regis Toomey, Anita Page, Barbara Week, Robert Ellis, Wheeler Oakman, Barbara Barondess, Dewey Robinson, George Cooper, Arthur Wanzer, Henry Wadsworth.

The Big Cage—1933. Universal Pictures Corp. Carl Laemmle, President. *Distributor:* Universal Pictures Corp. Sound (Western Electric Noiseless Recording). B&W. 8 reels. 71 or 75–77 min. *President:* Carl Laemmle. *Producer:* Carl Laemmle, Jr. *Director:* Kurt Neumann. *Script:* Edward Anthony and Ferdinand Reyher. *Adaptation:* Dale Van Every. *Additional Dialogue:* Clarence Marks. *Camera:* Goerge Robinson. *Film Editor:* Philip Cahn. *Cast:* Clyde Beatty, Anita Page, Andy Devine, Vince Barnett, Mickey Rooney, Wallace Ford, Raymond Hatton, Reginald Barlow, Edward Piel, Robert McWade, Wilfred Lucas, James Durkin.

Jungle Bride—1933. Monogram Pictures Corp. Trem Carr, Vice President in charge of production. *Distributor:* Monogram Pictures Corp. Sound. B&W. 7 reels, 5,632 feet. 63 min. Passed by the

National Board of Review. *President:* I.E. Chadwick. *Producer:* Arthur F. Beck. *Directors:* Harry O. Hoyt and Albert Kelley. *Assistant Director:* William Nolte. *Story:* Leah Baird. *Photography:* André Barlatier and Harry Jackson. *Art Director:* E.R. Hickson. *Film Editor:* Arthus Huffsmith. *Recording:* Homer Ellmaker. *Cast:* Anita Page, Charles Starrett, Kenneth Thompson, Eddie Borden, Clarence Geldert, Gertrude Simpson, Jay Emmett, Alfred Cross.

I **Have Lived**—1933. Chesterfield Motion Pictures Corporation. *Director:* Richard Thorpe. *Writing:* Winifred Dunn. *Cinematography:* M.A. Anderson. Also known as **After Midnight**. *Cast:* Gertrude Astor, Matthew Betz, Gladys Blake, Eddie Boland, Harry Bradley, Alan Dinehart, Florence Dudley, Dell Henderson, Anita Page, Maude Truax, Allen Vincent.

Hitch Hike to Heaven—1936. Invincible Pictures Corp. *Distributor:* Chesterfield Motion Pictures Corp. Sound. B&W. 7 reels. 63 min. *Producer:* Maury M. Cohen. *Supervisor:* Lon Young. *Director:* Frank R. Strayer. *Assistant Director:* Melville Shyer. *Story/Script:* Robert Ellis and Helen Logan. *Photography:* M.A. Andersen. *Film Editor:* Roland D. Reed. *Cast:* Henrietta Crosman, Herbert Rawlinson, Russell Gleason, Polly Ann Young, Al Shean, Anita Page, Syd Saylor, Harry Harvey, Harry Holman, Ethel Sykes, Lela Bliss, Crawford Kent, John Dilson.

Charles "Buddy" Rogers

Perhaps no other star during the twenties and early thirties epitomized the youth of America as much as Charles "Buddy" Rogers. It seems he was always the jest of a reviewer or writer for his endearing innocence and naiveté. There *were* others, certainly—among them David Rollins, Sue Carol, Churchill Ross, Arthur Lake and Eddie Quillan—who enjoyed great success in *The Collegians* film series. It was this type of film that perhaps best represented the Roaring Twenties and just how much fun everyone was having.

Charles "Buddy" Rogers was born on August 13, 1904, in Olathe, Kansas. His young three year old sister Geraldine couldn't pronounce "brother" but could manage "buddy"; hence, the nickname stuck and he was known around Olathe and eventually Hollywood as Buddy.

His father was editor of *The Olathe Mirror* weekly and it was in his dad's offices that the young boy did various errands and even had a route of 63 customers at age nine. And little Buddy had a musical bent also, playing in the Olathe Boys' Band. Jazz and band music would be a lifetime passion of his and he evolved into a fine musician as well as actor.

THE PARAMOUNT SCHOOL

It was while Charles was a student at the University of Kansas that his life took a path which led to eventual stardom. His father knew that talent scouts from Paramount Studios were in town and arranged through the owner of two local movie houses to get Buddy's picture and letters of recommendation into their hands.

"Paramount Pictures conducted a search for ten boys and ten girls from universities all over the country to go to a new school for acting in Astoria, New York. They came to Kansas University where I was a student [in journalism] and asked if I would like to try out. My father wanted me to do this so I agreed and was chosen to be one of the ten boys.

"Thelma Todd was one of the ten girls at the acting school in Astoria. We studied together and [we] were all friends. I started out with Paramount and stayed with them. They loaned me out to other studios for pictures. I made several pictures in England for different companies."

Buddy's father recalled his son's difficulty when he was at the Paramount School. In the 1929 July issue of *Photoplay*, he talks of this soon to be star in very endearing terms. "No one will ever know the heartaches that were Buddy's during the first few weeks of the six month term of the Paramount school.

"He was a shy, quiet, country boy whose experience was limited to a small town, save for his brief years at the university. He was made the butt of many ill-timed jokes and often referred to as the country kid or "Merton of the Movies" and I believe this had much to do with his appearing rather slow to learn."

Soon, however, Buddy received high praise for his performance in *Fascinating Youth* (1926), and "America's Boyfriend" was on the cusp of a major career. Initially praised more for his good looks than his acting, Buddy would land a goldmine role in *Wings* (1927). The industry had no choice but to stand up and take notice. A star was born, indeed.

"This was my first picture after arriving in California. I was introduced to [director] William Wellman who asked me to take one of the starring roles in *Wings*. Richard Arlen and I remained best friends until his death. Clara Bow was a close friend. We all got along great while filming! Gary Cooper was only in the picture for a few minutes but was a big hit. We remained friends.

"On location at Kelly Field in Texas while filming *Wings*, we sometimes had to wait days for the clouds to be just right to continue filming the air scenes. Conditions were a lot different than they are when filming today."

Buddy *was* the butt of jokes in his early career. Hollywood found it difficult perhaps to believe there could exist an innocent amongst the heathens and poked fun at him with no serious intent. The November 1928 issue of *Motion Picture* magazine carried a comical glib:

Sincerely,
Charles Rogers
Paramount Studios

"America's Boyfriend," Charles "Buddy" Rogers.

Top: Buddy at age nine, playing the trombone in The Olathe Boys' Band. He is third from the left; second row from the top. *Bottom:* John Powell (Buddy Rogers) comforts his dying pal, David Armstrong (Richard Arlen) in *Wings* (1927, Paramount).

"Clara Bow was entertaining a small and select audience with imitations of her fellow players. She opened her eyes very wide and stared at them with an expression of blank innocence. 'Beer?' she asked, 'What is beer?' ... 'Buddy Rogers,' they guessed with one accord!"

But his fans loved him. The same magazine ran an editorial by one Miss Dorothy Martin. She begs for more Buddy. "Why not give us young 'uns a great big hand? Give us more pictures that deal with our own particular joys and sorrows. In other words, give us youth and the joy of living that goes with it! Let's have some more men like Buddy Rogers. We're not jazz mad as people say we are, we're just chock full of the joy of living."

Enjoying Success ... and Mary

"We socialized mostly with other actors. We would attend [black-tie] dances at hotels like The Baltimore where we could cut in and dance with stars such as Mary Pickford [later his wife], Norma Shearer, etc. We were, at the time, a pretty close knit group. We also spent time together at Malibu at the beach. There were a lot of parties at different stars' homes.

"Mary Pickford was a real pro in the movie business. She knew every phase. She offered me the starring role opposite her in *My Best Girl* [1927]. She was great to work with and we became friends. I did not know Douglas Fairbanks, Sr., and only saw him a few times on the set of *My Best Girl* and at different social functions I attended at Pickfair. Of course after I married Mary I lived there for forty-three years until her death and until I sold Pickfair. Douglas Fairbanks, Jr., was one of my closest friends and remains so today.

"Yes, *Wings*, the picture I made with Clara Bow and Richard Arlen, won the first Academy Award. I attended the ceremonies. No one realized how important the Academy Awards would become!

"*Everything* [was] so different! William Wellman was my favorite director. He was one of the very best, really remarkable. I had very good luck with co-workers. All were talented and most remained good friends of mine.

"We were all saddened by [Valentino's] death. There was an air of disbelief and sorrow. We were all unsure as to whether we had 'voices.' Jack Oakie, Richard Arlen, Gary Cooper and I made a pact that if one of us did not have a 'voice' [for talkies], the others would give him ten percent of our earnings. Luckily we all had *voices*!

Buddy Rogers with wife Mary Pickford, London, 1964.

"Silents were wonderful to make. You have to make do with gestures and facial features. Sound movies were where most of my career was spent. I only made three silent films. I remember the [klieg] lights being hot and uncomfortable."

Buddy Rogers' career has lasted a long time. The silent film, talkies, his love for music would all show new facets in an evolving career. Perhaps his greatest achievement would be to remain a devoted and loving spouse to his wife, Mary Pickford.

And how would *he* like to be remembered? "As a competent actor and as a loyal friend to my co-workers. And as a very grateful actor to my fans.

"It was the greatest time to make movies, very glamorous and *fun*. Not at all like today, Thank God!"

FILMOGRAPHY

So's Your Old Man—1926. Famous Players. *Director:* Gregory LaCava. *Cast:* W. C. Fields, Alice Joyce, Charles "Buddy" Rogers, Kittens Reichert, Marcia Harris, Julia Ralph, Frank Montgomery, Jerry Sinclair.

More Pay-Less Work—1926. Fox Film Corp. *Director:* Albert Ray. *Writers:* Peter B. Kyne, Rex Taylor. *Cinematography:* Sidney Wagner. *Cast:* Albert Gran, Mary Brian, E.J. Ratcliffe, Charles "Buddy" Rogers. Otto Hoffman, Heinie Conklin, Frank Cooley.

Fascinating Youth—1926. Famous Players Lasky Corp. *Director:* Sam Wood. *Writers:* Byron Morgan, Paul Schofield. *Cinematography:* Leo Tover. *Cast:* Charles "Buddy" Rogers, Ivy Harris, Jack Luden, Walter Goss, Claude Buchanan, Mona Palma, Thelma Todd, Josephine Dunn, Thelda Kenvin, Jeanne Morgan, Dorothy Nourse, Irving Hartley, Gregory Blackton, Robert Andrews, Charles Brokaw, Iris Gray, Ralph Lewis, Joseph Burke, James Bradbury, Sr., Harry Sweet, William Black, Richard Dix, Adolphe Menjou, Clara Bow, Lois Wilson, Percy Marmont, Chester Conklin, Thomas Meighan, Lila Lee, Lewis Milestone, Malcolm St. Clair.

Wings—1927. Paramount Famous Lasky Corp. B&W. 35mm. 13 reels, 12,267 feet. *Director:* William A. Wellman. *Story:* John Monk Saunders. *Photography:* Harry Perry. *Additional Photography:* E. Burton Steen, Cliff Blackston, Russell Harland, Burt Baldridge, Frank Cotner, Faxon M. Dean,

Ray Olsen, Herman Schoop, L. Guy Wilky, Al Williams. *Music:* J.S. Zamecnik. *Cast:* Clara Bow, Charles "Buddy" Rogers, Richard Arlen, Jobyna Ralston, Gary Cooper, Arlette Marchal, El Brendel, Gunboat Smith, Richard Tucker, Julia Swayne Gordon, Henry B. Walthall, George Irving, Hedda Hopper, Nygil Debrulier, Dick Grace, Rod Rogers.

Get Your Man—1927. Paramount Famous Lasky Corp. *Director:* Dorothy Arzner. *Writers:* Agnes Brand Leahy, Hope Loring, George Marion, Jr., Louis Verneuil. *Cinematography:* Alfred Gilks. *Cast:* Clara Bow, Charles "Buddy" Rogers, Josef Swickard, Josephine Dunn, Harvey Clarke, Frances Raymond.

My Best Girl—1927. Mary Pickford Corp. *Distributor:* United Artists. B&W. 35mm. 9 reels, 7460 feet. *Director:* Sam Taylor. *Photography:* Charles Rosher. *Cast:* Mary Pickford, Charles "Buddy" Rogers, Sunshine Hart, Lucien Littlefield, Carmelita Geraghty, Hobart Bosworth, Evelyn Paul, Avonne Taylor, Mack Swain, Frank Finch Smiles, William Courtwright, John Junior, Harry Walker.

Red Lips—1928. Universal Pictures Corp. (also known as **The Plastic Age**). *Director:* Melville W. Brown. *Writers:* Melville W. Brown, James T. O'Donohoe, Percy Marks, Tom Reed. *Cinematography:* John Stumar. *Cast:* Marian Nixon, Charles "Buddy" Rogers, Stanley Taylor, Hayden Stevenson, Andy Devine, Robert Seiter, Hugh Trevor, Earl McCarthy.

Varsity—1928. Paramount Famous Lasky Corp. Talking Sequences/ Sound Effects/Music Score (Movietone). B&W. 8 reels, 6,348 feet. *Director:* Frank Tuttle. *Screenplay:* Howard Estabrook. *Photography:* A. J. Stout. *Film Editor:* Verna Willis. *Cast:* Charles "Buddy" Rogers, Mary Brian, Chester Conklin, Phillips R. Holmes, Rogert Ellis, John Westwood.

Someone to Love—1928. Paramount Famous Lasky Corp. Silent. B&W. 35mm. 7 reels, 6,323 feet. *Director:* F. Richard Jones. *Screenplay:* Keene Thompson, Monte Brice. *Photography:* Allen Siegler. *Cast:* Charles "Buddy" Rogers, Mary Brian, William Austin, Jack Oakie, James Kirkwood, Mary Alden, Frank Reicher.

River of Romance—1929. Paramount Famous Lasky Corp. Sound (Movietone). B&W. 35mm. 8 reels, 7,009 feet. *Director:* Richard Wallace. *Screenplay:* Ethel Doherty. *Title:* Joseph Mankiewicz. *Photography:* Victor Milner. *Film Editor:* Allyson Shaffer. *Cast:* Charles "Buddy" Rogers, Mary Brian , June Collyer, Henry B. Walthall, Wallace Beery, Fred Kholer, Natalie Kingston, Walter McGrail, Anderson Lawler, Mrs. George Fawcett, George Reed.

Perfect Day—1929. Hal Roach Studio/MGM. *Director:* James Parrott. *Writers:* Hal Roach, H.M. Walker, Leo McCarey. *Cast:* Stan Laurel, Oliver Hardy, Edgar Kennedy, Kay Deslys, Isabell Keith, Harry Bernard, Baldwin Cooke, Clara Guiol, Charles "Buddy" Rogers, Lyle Tayo.

Illusion—1929. Paramount Famous Lasky Corp. Sound. B&W. 35mm. 8 reels, 7,536 feet. *Director:* Lothar Mendes. *Photography:* Harry

Fischbeck. *Cast:* Charles "Buddy" Rogers, Nancy Carroll, June Collyer, Regis Toomey, Knute Erickson, K. Francis, Eugenie Besserer, Maude Turner Gordon, William Austin, Emilie Melville, Frances Raymond, Catherine Wallace, J. E. Nash, William McLaughlin, Eddie Payne, Michael Visaroll, Paul Lucas, Richard Cramer, Bessie Lyle, Col. G. L. McDonell, Lillian Roth, Harriet Spiker, Anna Magruder, Albert Wolffe.

Halfway to Heaven—1929. Paramount Famous Lasky Corp. Sound. B&W. 35mm. 8 reels, 6,254 feet. (Also silent, 5,179 ft). *Director:* George Abbott. *Photography:* Alfred Gilks, Charles Lang. *Cast:* Charles "Buddy" Rogers, Jean Arthur, Paul Lukas, Helen Ware, Oscar Apfel, Edna West, Irving Bacon, Al Hill, Lucille Williams, Richard K. French, Freddie Anderson, Nestor Aber, Ford West, Guy Oliver.

Close Harmony—1929. Paramount Famous Lasky Corp. Sound. B&W. 35mm. 7 reels, 6,271 feet. *Directors:* John Cromwell, Edward Sutherland. *Photography:* J. Roy Hunt. *Film Editor:* Tay Malarkey. *Cast:* Charles "Buddy" Rogers, Nancy Carroll, Harry Green, Jack Oakie, Richard "Skeets" Gallagher, Matty Roubert, Ricca Allen, Wade Boteler, Baby Mack, Oscar Smith, Greta Granstedt, Gus Partos, Jessee Stafford and His Orchestra.

Abie's Irish Rose—1929. Paramount Famous Lasky Corp. Talking Sequences/Sound Effects/Music Score: (Movietone). B&W. 35mm. 12 reels, 10,471 feet. (Also Silent 10,187 feet.) *Associate Producer:* B.P. Schulberg. *Director:* Victor Fleming. *Title:* Anne Nichols, Herman Mankiewicz, Julian Johnson. *Photography:* Harold Rosson. *Cast:* Charles "Buddy" Rogers, Nancy Carroll, Jean Hersholt, J. Farrell MacDonald, Bernard Gorcey, Ida Kramer, Nick Cogley, Camillus Pretal, Rosa Roasnova.

Young Eagles—1930. Paramount Famous Lasky Corp. Sound (Movietone). B&W 35mm. 8 reels, 6,406 feet. (Also Silent 6,710 feet.) *Director:* William A Wellman. *Photography:* A.J. Adrian, Leo Silesu. *Cast:* Charles "Buddy" Rogers, Jean Arthur, Paul Lukas, Stuart Erwin, Virginia Bruce, Gordon DeMain, James Finlayson, Frank Ross, Jack Luden, Freeman Wood, George Irving, Stanley Blystone, Newell Chase, Lloyd Whitlock.

Safety in Numbers—1930. Paramount-Publix Corp. Sound (Movietone). B&W. 35mm. 10 reels, 7,074 feet. *Director:* Victor Schertzinger. *Cast:* Charles "Buddy" Rogers, Kathryn Crawford, Josephine Dunn, Geneva Mitchell, Roscoe Karns, Francis McDonald, Virginia Bruce, Raoul Paoli, Louise Beavers, Richard Tucker.

Heads Up—1930. Paramount-Publix Corp. Sound (Movietone). B&W. 35mm. 9 reels, 6,785 feet. *Director:* Victor Schertzinger. *Photography:* William Steiner. *Cast:* Charles "Buddy" Rogers, Victor Moore, Helen Kane, Margaret Breen, Helen Carrington, Gene Cowing, Billy Taylor, Harry Shannon, C. Anthony Hughes, John Hamilton, Stanley Jessup, Preston Foster.

Paramount on Parade—1930. Paramount Famous Lasky Corp. Sound (Movietone). B&W with Color

Sequences (Technicolor). 35mm. 13 reels, 9,125 feet. *Directors:* Dorothy Arzner, Otto Brower, Edmund Goulding, Victor Heerman, Edwin H. Knopf, Rowland V. Lee, Ernst Lubitsch, Lothar Mendes, Victor Schertziner, Edward Sutherland, Frank Tuttle. *Photography:* Harry Fischbeck, Victor Milner. *Writer:* Joseph L. Mankiewicz. *Cast:* Iris Adrian, Richard Arlen, Jean Arthur, Mischa Auer, William Austin, George Bancroft, Clara Bow, Evelyn Brent, Mary Brian, Clive Brook, Virginia Bruce, Nancy Carroll, Ruth Chatterton, Maurice Chevalier, Gary Cooper, Cecil Cunningham, Leon Errol, Stuart Erwin, Henry Fink, Kay Francis, Richard "Skeets" Gallagher, Edmund Goulding, Harry Green, Mitzi Green, Robert Greig, James Hall, Phillips Holmes, Helen Kane, Dennis King, Abe Lyman and His Band, Fredric March, Nino Martni, Mitzi Mayfair, Marion Morgan Dancers, David Newell, Jack Oakie, Warner Oland, Zelma O'Neal, Eugene Pallette, Joan Peers, Jack Pennick, William Powell, Charles "Buddy" Rogers, Lillian Roth, Jackie Searl, Rolfe Sedan, Stanley Smith, Fay Wray.

Outside the Law—1930. Universal Pictures. *Director:* Tod Browning. *Writing:* Tod Browning, Garrett Fort. *Cinematography:* Roy F. Overbaugh. *Music:* David Broekman. *Cast:* Edward G. Robinson, Mary Nolan, Owen Moore, Eddie Sturgis, John George, Delmar Watson, DeWitt Jennings, Rockliff Fellowes, Frank Burke, Sidney Bracey, Rose Plummer, Louise Beavers, Matthew Betz, Charles "Buddy" Rogers, James B. Leong, Rodney Hildebrand, Frederick Burt.

Follow Thru—1930. Paramount-Publix Corp. Sound (Movietone), Color (Technicolor). 35mm. 10 reels, 8,386 feet. *Director/Screenplay:* Laurence Schwab, Lloyd Corrigan. *Photography:* Henry Gerrard, Charles Boyle. *Cast:* Charles "Buddy" Rogers, Nancy Carroll, Zelma O'Neal, Jack Haley, Eugene Pallette, Kathryn Givney, Margaret Lee, Don Tomkins, Albert Gran.

Along Came Youth—1930. Paramount/Publix Corp. Sound (Movietone). B&W. 35mm. 9 reels, 6,623 feet. *Director:* Lloyd Corrigan, Norman McLeod. *Photography:* Henry Gerrard. *Cast:* Charles "Buddy" Rogers, Frances Dee, Stuart Erwin, William Austin, Evelyn Hall, Leo White, Mathilde Comont, Betty Boyd, Arthur Hoyt, Sybil Grove, Herbert Sherwood, Charles West, Macon Jones, Billy Wheaton, George Ernest, Gordon Thorpe, John Strauss.

The Lawyer's Secret—1931. Paramount Publix Corp. *Distributor:* Paramount Publix Corp. Sound (Western Electric Noiseless Recording). B&W. 5,642 feet. 63 or 70 min. Passed by the National Board of Review. *Directors:* Louis Gasnier and Max Marcin. *Writer:* James Hilary Finn. *Photography:* Arthur Todd. *Cast:* Clive Brook, Charles "Buddy" Rogers, Richard Arlen, Fay Wray, Jean Arthur, Francis McDonald, Harold Goodwin, Syd Saylor, Laurence LaMarr, Robert Perry, Wilbur Mack.

Working Girls—1931. Paramount Publix Corp. *Distributor:* Paramount Publix Corp. Sound (Western Electric Noiseless Recording). B&W. 9 reels, 77 min. *Director:* Dorothy Arzner. *Photography:* Harry Fischbeck. *Cast:* Judith Wood, Dorothy Hall, Charles "Buddy" Rogers, Paul Lukas, Stuart Erwin, Frances Dee, Marjorie Gateson, Virginia Hammond, Mary Forbes, Frances Moffett, Claire Dodd, Dorothy Stickney, Alberta Vaughn, David Mir, Stella Moore, Gretta Gould, Mischa Auer.

The Road to Reno—1931. Paramount Publix Corp. *Distributor:* Paramount Publix Corp. Sound (Western Electric Noiseless recording). B&W. 8 reels. 73–74 min. Passed by the National Board of Review. *Director:* Richard Wallace. *Story:* Virginia Kellogg. *Writer:* Josephine Lovett. *Cast:* Lilyan Tashman, Charles "Buddy" Rogers, Peggy Shannon, William Boyd, Irving Pichel, Wynne Gibson, Skeets Gallagher, Tom Douglas, Judith Wood, Leni Stengel, Emile Chautard.

The Slippery Pearls—1931. National Variety Artists/Masquers Club of Hollywood/Butcher's Film Service (UK). (Also known as **The Stolen Jools**.) *Director:* William C. McGann. *Cast:* Joe E. Brown, Joan Crawford, Oliver Hardy, George "Gabby" Hayes, Eddie Kane, Buster Keaton, Stan Laurel, Edward G. Robinson, Norma Shearer, Allen "Farina" Hoskins, Matthew "Stymie" Beard, Norman "Chubby" Chaney, Bobby "Wheezer" Hutchins, Mary Ann Jackson, Shirley Jean Rickert, Dorothy DeBorba, "Little Billy" Rhodes, Polly Moran, Charles Murray, George Sidney, Charles "Buddy" Rogers, Jack Hill, J. Farrell MacDonald, Robert Ames, Richard Barthelmess, Warner Baxter, Wallace Beery, El Brendel, Charles Butterworth, Maurice Chevalier, Gary Cooper, Fifi D'Orsay, Bebe Daniels, Claudia Dell, Richard Dix, Irene Dunne, Douglas Fairbanks, Jr., Frank Fay, Louise Fazenda, Wynne Gibson, Mitzi Green, William Haines, Hedda Hopper, Winnie Lightner, Edmund Lowe, Ben Lyon, Victor McLaglen, Jack Oakie, Eugene Pallette, Lowell Sherman, Barbara Stanwyck, George E. Stone, Bert Wheeler, Robert Woolsey, Fay Wray, Loretta Young.

This Reckless Age—1932. Paramount Publix Corp. *Distributor:* Paramount Publix Corp. Sound (Western Electric Noiseless Recording). B&W. 8 reels. 63, 76 or 80 min. *Director:* Frank Tuttle. *Writers:* Lewis Beach, Frank Tuttle. (*Script:* Joseph L. Mankiewicz). *Photography:* Henry Sharp. *Cast:* Charles "Buddy" Rogers, Richard Bennet, Peggy Shannon, Charlie Ruggles, Frances Dee, Frances Starr, Maude Eburne, Allen Vincent, Mary Carlisle, David Landu, Reginald Barlow, George Pearce, Grady Sutton, Harry Templeton, Leonard Carey.

Take a Chance—1933. Paramount Productions, Inc. *Distributor:* Paramount Productions Inc. Western Electric Noiseless Recording. B&W. 9 reels. 80 min. *Directors:* Monte Brice and Laurence Schwab. *Photography:* Joseph Valentine and William Steiner. *Cast:* James Dunn, June Knight, Lillian Roth, Cliff Edwards,

Lillian Bond, Dorothy Lee, Lona Andre, Charles "Buddy" Rogers, Charles Richman, Robert Gleckler, George McKay.

Best of Enemies—1933. Fox Film Corp. *Distributor:* Fox Film Corp. Sound: (Western Electric Noiseless Recording). B&W. 8 reels, 6,800 feet. 71–72 min. *Directors:* Rian James and Frank Craven. *Writer:* Sam Mintz. *Photography:* L.W. O'Connell. *Cast:* Charles "Buddy" Rogers, Marian Nixon, Frank Morgan, Greta Nissen, Joseph Cawthorn, Arno Frey, W. E. Lawrence, Anders Van Haden.

Rambling 'Round Radio Row— 1933. Vitaphone/Warner Bros. *Director:* Jerry Wald. *Writer:* Jerry Wald. *Cinematography:* Edwin B. DuPar. *Cast:* Jerry Wald, Harry Rose, Bon Bon, Don Carney, Lew Conrad, John "Slim" Furness, Harriet Lee, Bob Pease, Charles "Buddy" Rogers.

Maid in Hollywood—1934. Hal Roach Studio. *Director:* Gus Meins. *Music:* Leroy Shield. *Cast:* Thelma Todd, Patsy Kelly, Eddie Foy, Jr., Don Barclay, Alphonse Martell, Charlie Hall, James C. Morton, Charles "Buddy" Rogers, Billy Bletcher, Ted Stroback. Carlton Griffin, Constance Bergen, Jack Barty, Billy Nelson.

I'll Be Suing You—1934. Hal Roach Studio. *Director:* Gus Meins. *Cast:* Thelma Todd, Patsy Kelly, Eddie Foy, Jr., Douglas Wakefield, Billy Neslon, Benny Baker, Charles "Buddy" Rogers, Charles McAvoy, William Wagner, Fred Kelsey.

Weekend Millionaire—1935. *Director:* Arthur B. Woods. *Writer:* Jack Davies, Geoffrey Kerr, Max Kester. *Cinematography:* Ronald Neame.

Cast: W. H. Berry, Mary Brian, Charles Carson, Norah Gale, Jimmy Godden, John Harwood, Iris Hoey, Aubrey Mallalieu, Nadine March, Billy Milton, Charles "Buddy" Rogers, Veronica Rose, Reginald Smith.

Pirate Party on Catalina Isle—1935. MGM. *Writer:* Alexander Van Horn. *Cinematography:* Ray Rennahan. *Cast:* Charles "Buddy" Rogers, Sterling Young, Robert Armstrong, Vince Barnett, Jack Duffy, Blanche Mehaffey, Bill Casper, Rue Tyler, Virginia Bruce, Betty Burgess, Lili Damita, Marian Davies, Johnny Downs, Leon Errol, Cary Grant, Chester Morris, Eddie Peabody, Mickey Rooney, Randolph Scott, Sid Silvers, Lee Tracy.

Dance Band—1935. British International. *Director:* Marcel Varnel. *Writers:* Roger Burford, Jack Davies, Dennis Waldock. *Cinematography:* Bryan Langley. *Music:* Harry Acres. *Cast:* Charles "Buddy" Rogers, June Clyde, Fred Duprez, Steven Geray, Hal Gordon, Fred Groves, Richard Hearne, Magda Kun, Albert Whelan.

Once in a Million—1936. *Director:* Arthur B. Woods. *Writers:* Jack Davies, Geoffrey Kerr, Max Kester. *Cinematography:* Ronald Neame, *Cast:* Mary Brian, Charles Carson, Jimmy Godden, John Harwood, Iris Hoey, Aubrey Mallalieu, Nadine March, Billy Milton, Charles "Buddy" Rogers, Veronica Rose, Reginald Smith.

Let's Make a Night of It—1937. Associated British Picture Corp. *Directors:* Graham Cutts, Walter C. Mycroft. *Writers:* Hugh Brooke, F. McGrew Willis. *Cinematography:*

Claude Friese-Greene, Otto Kanturek. Music Harry Acres. *Cast:* Charles "Buddy" Rogers, June Clyde, Claire Luce, Fred Emney, Iris Hoey, Jack Melford, Claud Allister, Steven Geray, Antony Holles, Lawrence Anderson, Zelma O'Neal, Bertha Belmore, Syd Wakefield, Dan Donovan, Brian Miche.

Golden Hoofs—1941. 20th Century–Fox. *Director:* Lynn Shores. *Writers:* Roy Chanslor, Ben Grauman Kohn, Thomas Langan. *Music:* Syril J. Mockridge. *Cinematography:* Lucien N. Andriot. *Cast:* Jane Withers, Charles "Buddy" Rogers, Kay Aldridge, George Irving, Buddy Pepper, Cliff Clark, Philip Hurlic, Sheila Ryan, Howard C. Hickman.

Double Trouble—1941. Monogram Pictures. *Director:* William West. *Writer:* Jack Natteford. *Music:* Ross DiMaggio. *Cinematography:* Arthur Martinelli. *Cast:* Betty Blythe, Louise Currie, Frank Jaquet, Edward Keane, Harry Langdon, Catherine Lewis, Billy Mauch, Mira McKinney, Dave O'Brien, Wheeler Oakman, Charles "Buddy" Rogers, Benny Rubin.

Mexican Spitfire's Baby—1941. RKO Radio Pictures. *Director:* Leslie Goodwins. *Writers:* Jerome Cady, Charles E. Roberts. *Music:* C. Bakaleinikoff. *Cinematography:* Jack MacKenzie. *Cast:* Lupe Velez, Leon Errol, Charles "Buddy" Rogers, ZaSu Pitts, Elizabeth Risdon, Fritz Feld, Marian Martin, Lloyd Corrigan, Lydia Bilbrook, Vinton Haworth, Jack Briggs, Jack Gardner, Jack Grey, James Harrison, Tom Kennedy, Donald Kerr,

Buddy Messinger, Ted O'Shea, Jane Patten, Dick Rush, Chester Tallman, Max Wagner, Jane Woodworth.

They Raid by Night—1942. Producers Releasing Corp. *Director:* Spencer Gordon Bennet. *Writer:* Jack Natteford. *Music:* David Chudnow. *Cinematography:* Gilbert Warrenton. *Cast:* John Beck, Swen Hugo Borg, Leslie Denison, June Duprez, Bruce Kellogg, Pierce Lyden, George N. Neise, Charles "Buddy" Rogers, Lyle Talbot, Sigfrid Tor, Victor Varconi, Crane Whitley, Eric Wilton.

Sing for Your Supper—1942. Columbia Pictures. *Director:* Charles Barton. *Writer:* Harry Rebuas. *Cinematography:* Franz Planer. *Cast:* Eve Arden, Sig Arno, Benny Baker, Harry Barris, Don Beddoe, Lloyd Bridges, Betty Brooks, Eddie Bruce, Earle D. Bunn, Eve Carlton, Dona Dax, Franchon Estes, Jinx Falkenburg, Dink Freeman, Burt Gordon, Berni Gould, Mildred Gover, Valerie Gratton, Bernadene Hayes, Earle Hodgins, Jessie May Jackson, Patricia Knox, Henry Kolker, Harry Lang, Perc Launders, Judith Linden, Larry Parks, Virginia Pherrin, Don Porter, Dewey Robinson, Charles "Buddy" Rogers, Walter Sande, Luise Squire, Red Stanley, Dorothy Trail, Glen Turnbull.

Mexican Spitfire Sees a Ghost—1942. RKO Radio Pictures. *Director:* Leslie Goodwins. *Writer:* Monte Brice, Charles E. Roberts. *Music:* C. Bakaleinikoff. *Cinematography:* Russell Metty. *Cast:* Lupe Velez, Leon Errol, Charles "Buddy" Rogers, Elizabeth Risdon,

Donald MacBride, Minna Gombell, Don Barclay, John Maguire, Lillian Randolph, Mantan Moreland, Harry Tyler, Marten Lamont, Richard Martin, Linda Rivas, Sally Wadsworth, Julie Warren, Jane Woodworth.

Mexican Spitfire at Sea—1942. RKO Radio Pictures. *Director:* Leslie Goodwins. *Writers:* Jerome Cady, Charles E. Roberts. *Music:* C. Bakaleinikoff. *Cinematography:* Jack MacKenzie. *Cast:* Lupe Velez, Leon Errol, Charles "Buddy" Rogers, ZaSu Pitts, Elizabeth Risdon, Florence Bates, Marian Martin, Lydia Bilbrook, Eddie Dunn, Harry Holman, Marten Lamont, Lou Davis, Mary Field, Warren Jackson, John Maguire, Richard Marten, Wayne McCoy, Ferris Taylor, Julie Warren.

House of Errors—1942. Producers Releasing Corp. *Director:* Bernard B. Ray. *Writers:* Ewart Adamson, Eddie Davis, Harry Langdon. *Music:* Lee Zahler. *Cast:* Betty Blythe, Roy Butler, Ed Cassidy, Vernon Dent, Gwen Gaze, John Holland, Guy Kingsford, Harry Langdon, Marian Marsh, Charles "Buddy" Rogers, Ray Walker.

That Nazty Nuisance—1943. *Director:* Glenn Tryon. *Writers:* Clarence Marks, Earle Snell. *Music:* Edward Ward. *Cinematography:* Robert Pittack. *Cast:* Johnny Arthur, Joe Devlin, Rex Evans, Frank Faylen, Ian Keith, Ed Lewis, Wedgwood Nowell, Emory Parnell, Jean Porter, Charles 'Buddy' Rogers, Henry Victor, Bobby Watson.

An Innocent Affair—1948. United Artists. *Director:* Lloyd Bacon (also known as **Don't Trust Your Husband**). *Writers:* Lou Breslow, Joseph Hoffman. *Music:* Hans J. Salter. *Cinematography:* Edward Cronjager. *Cast:* Louise Allbritton, Marie Blake, Madeleine Carroll, Rita Johnson, Eddie Le Baron, Fred Mac Murray, Matt McHugh, Susan Miller, Alan Mowbray, Anne Nagel, Charles "Buddy" Rogers, Mike Romanoff, James Seay, William Tannen, Pierre Watkin, Jane Weeks.

David Rollins

David Rollins liked being in the movies. His enthusiasm when we talked on the phone shed volumes about his early career and how important it had been to him. Of course it didn't hurt that he had "all–American boy" good looks and no doubt caught the eye of the studios.

David modestly downplayed his physical attributes but admitted that "it got one past the closed gates of the studio and in contact with directors and people who mattered [such as] heads of the studios. It was harder in those days [to become a film star]. Everyone in those days wanted a career in films."

Still, one had to have talent and the ability to act for the camera. "We were young people with youth, beauty, personality and *talent*. Getting inside the studio then, you had to know somebody, you had to be there for some reason. You sometimes had to pay somebody to get in but if you knew somebody like Gary Cooper or Charlie Farrell, yes, he would always let them in. It was hard in those days to get somewhere. It was very difficult.

"Somebody had to watch you [or] say whether you had talent or a pretty face or whatever." David Rollins not only succeeded in silents where he eventually was contracted with Fox Studio, but also weathered the storm from silent films to talkies, a dark time for Hollywood when many actors faced looming unemployment because of their vocal quality and early problems with sound pictures.

INSIDE THE GATES

Once David had achieved his initial success in films, he quickly learned that the actor was, in part, property of the studio. "There was

162

David Rollins at the summit of his career (photo credit: Lansing Brown).

a morality clause in every contract. In your personal life you were told what you could do and couldn't do that might hurt your movie image.

"If you did anything they [the studio] didn't like, they could cancel your contract immediately, automatically. That's why they had a moral clause. There *were* scandals. There were people that took dope and there were people that got mixed up sexually with people like the [Fatty] Arbuckle case. All kinds of things, life was just the same then as it is now. [Roscoe "Fatty" Arbuckle was alleged to have raped and killed a young woman in 1921, Virginia Rappe. He was later acquitted but the publicity ruined his career, and as a result, studio heads and their players were put under the microscope of Will Hayes, Hollywood's father of the "morality clause."]

"But they [the actors] weren't under obligation, a lot of them. So they didn't have to tell everything, they didn't have to admit everything [before the code]. It was [easier] for those things to leak out because the publicity was so great. And people didn't know any better. They didn't know they weren't supposed to do this and supposed to do that.

"I was never a part of any of that, thank goodness. I witnessed two or three things that they said about Joan Crawford and oh ... things like that. I was too young to be allowed to go to parties, those kind of parties. I didn't drink, I didn't smoke [and] I didn't carry on. I wasn't tempted there [but] it was there if you wanted it. [Crawford] married Douglas Fairbanks, Jr., they said, for his money! But he didn't have any money then. It wasn't a very prosperous thing for her to marry [him] anyway. She could have had anybody.

"I used to go dancing at the Coconut Grove. They all had special places they went and were invited to. People like Lilyan Tashman [were there] but I never partied around with them. I was too young. They were looking for people their own age.

"Yes, it was a fun town. There were a lot of good places to go and be part of your own town."

Yet to some press people, David appeared to be somewhat of an enigma. Interviewer William H. McKegg described his association with David in the March 1930 issue of *Picture Play* magazine. "He's a strange fellow. Whenever he sees me he appears to be on the verge of telling me astounding things—but the talk is merely casual.

A debonair Rollins (note the dimple).

"In one of my articles I chaffed David about a massive ring he wore. Instead of continuing to wear it, or sport an even larger one, he discarded it. He had the power to turn the laugh on me, but he didn't do it. However, since then, after exchanging further views on this or that, we have a higher regard for each other than we possessed before.

"After meeting Mr. Rollins several more times, I may learn something about him to alter my present vague ideas. Of course, I don't promise to find out anything new. But David seems charged with revelations about to materialize. When that occurs he is going to progress in acting and will give us something to talk about. In the meantime I shall see him informally, with my other movie acquaintances, and that may reveal some traits in him worth recording."

MAKIN' MOVIES

David Rollins was one of the lucky ones. He survived the transition from silent films to talkies, unlike so many great actors who died a quiet death in front of the microphone. I asked David about the process of making a film and what, if any, training did the studio provide.

"I was up at 7 A.M.; makeup department, wardrobe department if necessary. On the set by 9 A.M. till 10 or 11 at night [and] sometimes even later if necessary.

"The studios all had dramatic schools. Louise Dresser [had] a class because she had been a stage actress for so many years and thought she'd be good and teach others how to act....

"She was a lovely person and was with my mother in two or three films. We went every morning at 9 A.M. and stayed with her until noon. She had us do certain scenes from Shakespeare or recite poems, just to get us talking.

"With Fox Studios, having lessons in voice, singing, diction, and dancing was necessary for one's current picture plans. They all [other studios] had dramatic schools. All the young people went. [If] the studio was happy with them, they put them into bits of pictures. That is how they [actors] started out. The studios did not want to take any chances either. That is why they'd have a clause in their contract to behave yourself.

"We were all put in schools. We were told what to do, how to talk, how to walk; that's one of the first things we used to do when we were taken under a contract. They would sort of prime you for anything."

What David Rollins may not have been primed for was yet to come. Acclaimed German director F. W. Murnau would become a close friend to David, even using him in two films. It was, however, Murnau's desire to see David in the nude which both puzzled and surprised him.

Murnau had had great success. His film credits included *Faust* (1926), *Sunrise* (1927) and *The Last Laugh* (1925). David recalled Murnau and his bizarre behavior but held no shame or bitterness.

"He was a great friend of mine. If he hadn't died, I would probably have worked with him more than I did. I was in only two of his pictures [but] he wanted to take me to the South Seas to make a [picture] about, oh what do you call it ... a boy that became a native....

"He had a yacht and he always wanted to take me on his yacht, to South Tahiti. He never asked me if I had permission to go. The studio just took it for granted that whatever he wanted to do, he could. So when I went for an interview with him for the first time, he said, 'take off your clothes.'

"He said, 'I am watching your legs,' so I took off my clothes and he just sat there and didn't say anything. He told me he was going to take me to the South Seas and I was to be ready at a certain hour at the corner of Hollywood Boulevard and Sunset to pick me up. A chauffeur approached and at the last minute, I got frightened and said, 'I'm not going with him.'

"He might be very strange [I thought], I don't know. So they started out and he [Murnau] said he waited for me for an hour. They took off and said, 'To hell with you,' I guess. They were on their way to San Francisco and he [Murnau's chauffeur] drove over a cliff, killing both of them. If I had been there, I would have been killed myself.

"I have always been told to take off my clothes here and there. I was never ashamed of my body. He wanted to see how I would look in the nude so I used to go take off my clothes and go for a swim at night. He used to come and watch. He said he had some trouble when he was in the army. It was some kind of shock or some kind of ... I don't know what it was, but it wasn't for sexual purposes.

"He said he just wanted to look at me. He never had any children of his own so he might have been like a couple of other directors that I had known. They wanted to adopt me."

David Rollins, circa 1932.

Marilyn Monroe of Her Day

David Rollins admitted he was smitten by another Hollywood superstar, Clara Bow. His affection for Bow was charming years later, and still as sincere.

"I loved her. She was a friend of mine and also her husband George Beldam and (later), Rex Bell. [Beldam started out as a stuntman for Fox Studio which later changed his name to Rex Bell.] Her boyfriend [Beldam] roomed next to me in the make-up department when they used to go together. I got to know him quite well and he wanted to know if I would meet her.

The "Marilyn Monroe of her day," Clara Bow, in 1930.

"So I met her one day and she was very nice. I had a car, a little Roadster and I named it CLARA BOW because it had wheels with the same color as her hair. We were very friendly and I knew her very well but I didn't go out with her socially. She was wonderful. She was the Marilyn Monroe of her day."

The Shift to Sound

"People were frightened that their voices might not be right for sound. Even people like John Gilbert who was a *big* star, he had a squeaky voice and he couldn't change it so they let him go. [The studios] automatically canceled you. It must have been devastating to him.

"The studio had me sing one day. They wanted to put me in a musical. If one could sing, good. If not? Too bad. Evidently I passed the test and I was in a musical with a girl called Sue Carol. We played around and got good notices about our voices. But it was said that some people's voices sounded like they were in a barrel somewhere. It was a long siege there for awhile until they all got adjusted."

One thing David Rollins definitely did *not* like was seeing himself on the big screen. I asked him what it was like the first time he saw his films.

"It wasn't me up there; it was somebody else. I never did like to see myself on the screen. I wasn't embarrassed [but] I just couldn't get used to it. They made me go and look at the rushes sometimes and I wasn't too happy with what I saw. The studio wanted to show me something I was doing, something they wanted to perfect. Maybe it was the way I spoke or whatever I was doing. I don't remember now, it's been so long."

And of all his Hollywood friends and co-workers during those pioneering years, who were some of his favorites? "Johnny Weismuller, he was a very close friend of mine. And Victor McLaughlin, Marion Morrison [later John Wayne], my former schoolmate. Arthur Lake, Myrna Loy, Lupe Velez ... the list goes on and on. Charles Paddock, very business like, still trying to get [his] Olympic medal! [Paddock won the 1920 Olympic Gold Medal for the one hundred meter run in Antwerp and later tried films.] Everybody in those days wanted a career in films."

But not everyone was as successful as David Rollins. Whether it was one of the delightful Collegian films, a musical or a comedy, David loved the camera and expressed no regrets. "It was just a great big different sort of life!"

FILMOGRAPHY

High School Hero—1927. Fox Film Corp. *Director:* David Butler. *Cinematography:* Ernest Palmer. *Writers:* David Butler, Seton I. Miller. *Cast:* Nick Stuart, Sally Phipps, William Bailey, John Darrow, Wade Boteler, Brandon Hurst, David Rollins, Charles Paddock.

Thanks for the Buggy Ride—1928. Universal. *Director:* William A. Seiter. *Cinematography:* Arthur L. Todd. *Writers:* Byron Morgan, Beatrice Van. *Cast:* Laura La Plante, Glenn Tyron, Richard Tucker, Kate Price, Jack Raymond, Trixie Friganza, Lee Moran, David Rollins.

Win That Girl—1928. Fox Film Corp. *Director:* David Butler. *Cinematography:* Glen MacWilliams. *Writers:* Dudley Early, John Stone.

Cast: David Rollins, Sue Carol, Tom Elliott, Roscoe Karns, Olin Francis, Mack Fluker, Sidney Bracey, Janet McLeod, Maxine Shelly, Betty Recklaw.

The Air Circus—1928. Fox Film Corp. *Directors:* Howard Hawks, Lewis Seiler. *Cinematography:* Daniel B. Clark. *Writers:* C. Graham Baker, Norman Z. McLeod. *Cast:* Arthur Lake, Sue Carol, David Rollins, Louise Dresser, Heinie Conklin, Charles Delaney, Earl Robinson II.

Prep and Pep—1928. Fox Film Corp. *Director:* David Butler. *Cinematographer:* Joseph A. Valentine, Sidney Wagner. *Writers:* Malcolm Stuart Boylan, John Stone. *Sound Effects and Musical Score:* Western Electric Sound System. *Cast:* David Rollins, Nancy Drexel, John Darrow, E.H. Calvert, Frank Albertson, Robert Peck.

Riley the Cop—1928. Fox Film Corp. *Director:* John Ford. *Cinematographer:* Charles G. Clarke. *Writers:* James Gruen, Fred Stanley. *Sound Effects and Musical Score:* Western Electric Sound System. *Cast:* J. Farrell MacDonald, Louise Fazenda, Nancy Drexel, David Rollins, Harry Schultz, Mildred Boyd, Ferdinand Schumann-Heink, Dell Henderson, Mike Donlin, Russ Powell, Tom Wilson, Billy Bevan, Otto Fries.

Why Leave Home?—1929. Fox Film Corp. *Director:* Raymond Cannon. *Cinematographer:* Daniel B. Clark. *Writers:* Robert S. Carr, Russell G. Medcraft and Norman Mitchell (play: *Cradle Snatchers*). *Original Music:* Con Conrad, Archie Gottler, Sidney D. Mitchell. *Sound Effects and Musical Score:* Western

Elec. Sound System. *Cast:* Sue Carol, Nick Stuart, Dixie Lee, Ilka Chase, Jean Bary, Walter Catlett, Gordon De Main, Dot Farley, Laura Hamilton, Richard Keene, Fred MacMurray, Jed Prouty, David Rollins.

Fox Movietone Follies of 1929—Fox Film Corp. *Director:* David Butler. *Cinematographer:* Charles Van Enger. *Writers:* David Butler, William K. Wells. *Music:* Con Conrad, Archie Gottler, Sidney D. Mitchell. MovieTone Sound Mix. *Cast:* Sue Carol, Sharon Lynn, Dixie Lee, Lola Lane, John Breeden, Robert Burns, Jackie Cooper, Melva Cornell, Jeanette Dancey, Mario Dominici, Stepin Fetchit, Vina Gale, Archie Gottler, John Griffith, Charles Huff, Helen Hunt III, Warren Hymer, DeWitt Jennings, Arthur Kay, Frank La Mont, Paula Langlen, Henry M. Mollandin, David Percey, Frank Richardson, David Rollins, Carolynne Snowden, Arthur Springer, Arthur Stone.

The Black Watch—1929. Fox Film Corp. *Director:* John Ford. *Writers:* James Kevin McGuinness, John Stone, Talbot Mundy. *Cinematographer:* Joseph H. August. *Music:* William Kernell. *Sound:* MovieTone. *Cast:* Victor McLaglen, Myrna Loy, Roy D'Arcy, Pat Somerset, David Rollins, Mitchell Lewis, Walter Long, David Percy, Lumsden Hare, Cyril Chadwick, David Torrence, Francis Ford, Claude King, Frederick Sullivan, Joseph Diskay, Joyzelle Joyner, Richard Travers, Randolph Scott, Mary Gordon, Jack Pennick, John Wayne.

Love, Live and Laugh—1929. Fox Film Corp. *Director:* William K.

Howard. *Writers:* Edwin J. Burke, Dana Burnet, Leroy Clemens, John B. Hymer, George Jessel. *Cinematographer:* Lucien N. Andriot. Western Electric Sound. *Cast:* George Jessel, Lila Lee, David Rollins, Harry Kolker, John Loder, John Reinhardt, Dick Winslow Johnson, Henry Armetta, Marcia Manon, Jerry Mandy.

Happy Days—1930. Fox Film Corp. *Director:* Benjamin Stoloff. *Writers:* Edwin J. Burke, Sidney Lanfield. *Cinematographer:* Lucien N. Androit, John Schmitz. J.O. Taylor. *Sound:* MovieTone. *Cast:* Charles E. Evans, Marjorie White, Richard Keene, Stuart Erwin, Martha Lee Sparks, Clifford Dempsey, James Corbett, George MacFarlane, Janey Gaynor, Charles Farrell, Victor McLaglen, El Brendel, William Collier, Sr., Tom Patricola, George Jessel, Dixie Lee, Nick Stuart, Rex Bell, Frank Albertson, Sharon Lynn, "Whispering" Jack Smith, Lew Brice, J. Farrell MacDonald, Will Rogers, Edmund Lowe, Walter Catlett, Frank Richardson, Ann Pennington, David Rollins, Warner Baxter, Helen Mann, Mary Lansing, Beverly Royed, Joan Navarro, Paul Page, Catherine Navarro, Dorothy McNames, Vee Maule, Hazel Sperling, Bo Peep Karlin, Georgia Pembleton, Marbeth Wright, Miriam Hellman, Margaret La Marr, Consuelo De Los Angeles, Lee Auburn, Betty Halsey, Joyce Lorme, Myra Mason, Eileen Bannon, Theresa Allen, Pear La Velle, Barbara La Velle, Gertrude Friedly, Dorothy Kirsten, Doris Baker, Melissa Ten Eyck, Kay Gordon, Betty Gordon, Jean De Parva, Joan Gaylord, Charlotte Hamill, Alice Goodsell, Gwen Keate, Virginia Joyce, LaVerne Leonard, Betty Grable, Marjorie Levoe, Pat Hanne, Estella Essex, Jack Frost, John Westerfelt, Douglas Steade, Peter Custulovich, John Lockhart, Randall Reynolds, Carter Sexton, Leo Hanley, George Scheller, Kenneth Nordyke, Marius Langan, Ralph Demaree, Glen Alden, Frank McKee, Joe Holland, Ed Rockwell, Clarence Brown, Jr., Roy Rockwood, Enrico Cuccinelli, Harry Lauder, Ted Waters, Thomas Vartian, J. Harold Reeves, Phil Kolar, Fran Heller, William Hargraves, Ted Smith III, Tom Kennedy, J. Harold Murray, George Olsen.

The Big Trail—1930. Fox Film Corp. *Directors:* Louis R. Loeffler, Raoul Walsh. *Writers:* Marie Boyle, Hal G. Evarts, Jack Peabody, Florence Postal. *Cinematographer:* Lucien N. Androit, Arthur Edeson. *Music:* Arthur Kay. *Sound:* MovieTone. *Cast:* John Wayne, Marguerite Churchill, El Brendel, Tully Marshall, Tyrone Power, Sr., David Rollins, Ian Keith, Frederick Burton, Russ Powell, Charles Stevens, Helen Parrish, Louise Carver, William V. Mong, Dodo Newton, Jack Peabody, Ward Bond, Marcia Harris, Marjorie Lee, Emslie Emerson, Frank Rainboth, Andy Shufford, Gertrude Van Lent, Lucille Van Lent, DeWitt Jennings, Alphonse Ethier, Chief John Big Tree, Andy Shuford.

Morals for Women—1931. (Also known as **Farewell Party**.) Tiffany

Productions. *Director:* Mort Blumenstock. *Writer:* Frances Hyland. *Cinematographer:* Max Dupont. *Cast:* Lina Basquette, Edmund Breese, June Clyde, Virginia Lee Corbin, Emma Dunn, John Holland, Bessie Love, Natalie Moorhead, David Rollins, Conway Tearle.

Mama Loves Papa—1931. Hal Roach Studios Inc./Metro-Goldwyn-Mayer. *Director:* George Stevens. *Producer:* Hal Roach. *Writer:* H.M. Walker. *Music:* Leroy Shield. *Cast:* Mickey Daniels, Grady Sutton, David Rollins, Mary Kornman, Gertrude Messinger, May Wallace, Harry Bernard, Charlie Hall.

Girls Demand Excitement—1931. Fox Film Corp. *Director:* Seymour Felix. *Writers:* Owen Davis, W. Robertson, Harry Sauber, Ray Harris, R. Medcraft. *Cinematographer:* Charles Clarke. *Cast:* Virginia Cherrill, John Wayne, Marguerite Churchill, Edward Nugent, Helen Jerome Eddy, Terrance Ray, Martha Sleeper, William Janney, Ralph Welles, George Irving, Winter Hall, Marion Byron, Emerson Treacy, Addie McPhail, Jerry Mandy, Ray Cooke, Carter Gibson, David Rollins.

The Kickoff—1931. Hal Roach/MGM. *Director:* George Stevens. *Producer:* Hal Roach. *Cast:* Harry Bernard, Betty Bolen, Mickey Daniels, Charlie Hall, Mary Kornman, David Rollins, Grady Sutton, Leo Willis.

Young Sinners—1931. Fox Film Corp. *Director:* John Blystone.

Cast: Thomas Meighan, Hardie Albright, Dorothy Jordan, Cecelia Loftus, James Kirkwood, Edmund Breese, Lucien Prival, Arnold Lucy, Nora Lane, Joan Castle, John Arledge, David Rollins, Edward Nugent, Billy Butts, Gaylord Pendleton, Yvonne Pelletier.

Probation—1932. (Also known as **Second Chances.**) Chesterfield Motion Picture Corp. *Director:* Richard Thorpe. *Writer:* Edward T. Lowe, Jr. *Cinematographer:* M.A. Anderson. *Cast:* Sally Blane, Betty Grable, Mary Jane Irving, Matty Kemp, J. Farrell MacDonald, Eddie Phillips, David Rollins, Clara Kimball Young.

Love Pains—1932. Hal Roach Studios/MGM. *Director:* James W. Horne. *Producer:* Hal Roach. *Cast:* Mickey Daniels, Grady Sutton, David Rollins, Mary Kornman, Betty Bolen, Harry Bernard, Blanche Payson, Gordon Douglas, Marvin Hatley, Shirley Jean Rickert.

The Phantom Express—1932. Majestic Pictures Inc. *Director:* Emory Johnson. *Writers:* Laird Doyle, Emory Johnson. *Cinematographer:* Ross Fisher. *Cast:* J. Farrell MacDonald, William Collier, Jr., Sally Blane, Axel Axelson, Eddie Phillips, David Rollins, Hobart Bosworth, Claire McDowell, Lina Basquette, Alice Dahl, Robert Ellis, Allan Forrest, Huntley Gordon, Dorothy Gulliver, Brady Kline, Robert Littlefield, Jack Mower, Tom O'Brien, Jack Pennick, Carl Stockdale, Jack Trent, Tom Wilson.

Andrew Stone

There very well may be another director somewhere out there who started out in silent films and continued right on through talkies until the early 1970s. But the only director I know of in such a category and who still lives in California is Andrew Stone.

Born in Oakland, California, on July 16, 1902, Andrew Stone spoke from his home to me and several follow-ups as well. What I discovered was a man of deep humility with a true sense of what he believed in and why he felt his career had lasted for decades. He is adamant in his opinions and speaks with a voice which still could command attention on a movie set.

When he first landed in Hollywood he started working in the film labs. "I worked in different departments; the drying room, one thing or another." He went on to direct his first film, *The Elegy* (1926). He had no tutor nor did he work under another director as an apprentice. The journey from the film labs to behind the camera, he exclaimed, "would take too long to tell over the phone!"

"I made my first silent picture in 1926, *The Elegy*, and it was a big hit with Tyrone Power, Sr., Phillipe de Lacy and Gladys Brockwell. I raised the money and made it independently. Paramount released it. Then I got a contract from Paramount to do three or four more films. I directed *every* picture I made in my life!

DAVID WARK GRIFFITH

Andrew Stone was also fortunate to have film editor Jimmy Smith with him in his early career. Smith was film editor to legendary director D.W. Griffith. Smith, Griffith and Griffith's cameraman Billy Bitzer blazed a long trail in the early development of films. With Bitzer's help, Griffith was credited for pioneering such film techniques as the close-up, the fade in and fade out, and also the art of the long shots.

"Jimmy Smith was very, very good, excellent! He was Griffith's editor on all his pictures in the early days and he was my editor [after he left Griffith]. Jimmy cut three of my pictures and was 'no nonsense.' Great!

"I didn't know him [Griffith] personally but we had many mutual friends. Griffith didn't advance with the times and he got washed up. His last couple of pictures were terrible—*The Sorrows of Satan* [1926] for example. He was still making old time pictures [and] was out of a job. He was *far* ahead of his time but did not advance in his concepts."

Early film star Henry Walthall remembered Griffith also. In an August 1931 interview in *New Movie Magazine*, Walthall, who played the Little Colonel in Griffith's classic *Birth of a Nation* (1915), spoke of Griffith.

"Mr. Griffith was a gay, happy man in those days and very democratic. He joined in all our pleasures when we went on location, such as sports, playing cards and dancing. He was always singing on the sets. And how he did work! We ourselves never knew *when* we'd be going to bed. We'd be called for nine in the morning and might meet ourselves coming to work the next morning.

"All this time Griffith was evolving new ideas for the screen. He and Billy Bitzer, his cameraman, used to go away on trips together. They would always come back with some new idea to be tried out on the screen."

Walthall, a stage actor, started in films during summers when he was out of work. "We only got five dollars a day anyhow. Most of us treated picture acting as a joke and a mere meal ticket. Yes, that was 1909."

LESS MAKEUP, MORE MUSIC

Andrew Stone weathered a remarkable transition from silents right up to the 1970s. A bit of a pioneer himself, and a rebel, he recalled the many differences he'd witnessed along his directorial journey.

"The cameraman and director played a bigger part during the silent era than in talking pictures. It took more skill to light black and white

Best wishes to Tony

Director Andrew Stone filming *The Last Voyage*, 1960.

films than colored pictures. The director could talk to the actors while filming to build emotion. There were a *lot* of differences between silents and talking films. The studio musicians were great and I really missed the studio orchestras, especially when it came to emotional scenes. The music helped tremendously. They were a big loss to the directors when sound came in.

"Subtitles were made by title companies and inserted by the editor. I have vivid memories of the klieg lights because I received a serious eye infection from them. It was extremely painful. But the studios managed to soften down the glare, so in later times they were okay.

"Putting makeup on, ridiculous, everything ridiculous. The makeup was preposterous! Through the silent pictures, they looked like they had masks on, most of them. They had bad makeup on stage plays, therefore they figured, 'Well, you need it in pictures.'

"I wouldn't permit makeup on any man in my pictures and I discouraged the women from using makeup. It was crazy."

The October 1921 edition of *Motion Picture* magazine reprinted the July 1913 "prophecy," at which time the industry held these statements as standards to which the art of the cinema would improve:

> #24. Talking pictures will not displace the silent drama, but better music and orchestral accompaniment will add to the effectiveness of motion pictures. The public will learn that anything that distracts from what the eye sees is not pleasurable, and that motion pictures are complete in themselves because words are not necessary and only retard the imagination.

> #25. The future will see better photography; not necessarily scenic, although this too, will be improved, but particularly, portraiture. The art of making-up for the pictures will be changed so that when a scene is properly lighted the face will not appear chalky white and expressionless and the lips black.

The insights of Andrew Stone concerning photography and "particularly, portraiture," prove he was indeed ahead of his time.

LOCATION WORK AND THE TALKIES

"I was the first to one hundred percent abandon the sheer nonsense of shooting in a studio and shot everything on natural locations. It took the industry ten years to catch up to me in this concept. I could get a whole house in Beverly Hills for one hundred dollars a day, a whole house! You'd shoot in the living room, dining room, kitchen, bedroom. When you looked out the window, you didn't look out to a blow up of a still photograph! Oh, don't get me started, I'll be on the phone all day!

"You could shoot later today than you could then. The lenses weren't fast then. A few of the independents like Nat Levine, who started Republic, really took advantage of the daylight. They'd start early in the morning and shoot till the sun went down at night. But I never did. I shot regular hours, nine in the morning to six at night. Except for Nat Levine, I think most of them shot from nine to six.

"The whole making of pictures of course, is ridiculous. I mean, building sets in the studio because they had sets on the first pictures!

"When sound first came in, the camera was in a soundproof box on wheels and you had to move it around. You couldn't shoot pan shots, dolly shots [a shot in which the camera moves while shooting] or anything.

"The bigger microphones had to be placed in potted plants and things. The sound engineers were way up in a booth near the ceilings. It was a whole different ball of wax."

Frank "Junior" Coghlan, one of Cecil B. DeMille's favorite child actors of the twenties, also remembers the pioneering changes from silent to sound. "Sound was new and they had mikes hidden behind books and other objects. The poor camera crew members were encased in a box-like structure and air conditioning, or any other form of cooling, was not available. However, they did a great job for us under these undesirable conditions. Silents were fun, but talkies much more demanding as we had to memorize lines."

Continued Stone: "There were a lot of people before talking pictures that would say, 'They'll never last!' I thought the people were *idiots* who said silent pictures were better. You'd be surprised in the late twenties, the people who said talkies wouldn't last, that they were just a fad. It was obvious! How could talkies compare with silent pictures where you had titles all the way through? It was ridiculous!"

Certainly part of the concern, at least from an actor's viewpoint, was *how* their voices would record. An article from the November 1928 issue of *Motion Picture* magazine is worth the reprint here for its humor and apparent wisdom as well.

A lot of new words are being heard around the studios these days. A *blooper*, for instance, is the possessor of a voice which blasts on the recording device. A *sizzler* generates vibrant sounds with his teeth so that he hisses himself. A *juice sucker* has a voice that whispers and must be amplified; while a *growler*, of course, speaks in gutturals, and a *corduroy voice* is one that wavers, now loud, now soft. The voice that records really well is called the *dynaphonic*, and how the girls and boys are praying for these is simply nobody's business!

Pola Negri

Silent film vamp Pola Negri made her American "comeback" in Andrew Stone's *Hi Diddle Diddle* (1943—also known as *Diamonds and Crime*). Negri had enjoyed great success in Germany after a less than thrilling entry into American sound films. And she would also be reunited with Adolphe Menjou, one of her silent film co-stars.

"Pola's agent sold me on the idea. She was wonderful to work with and we became very close friends. She was still a very big star but a very nice woman and a very good actress. There were no problems at all. And Menjou, Oh God, he was a dream. I had him for two pictures.

"Strangely enough, we hardly ever discussed the silent era. I don't know why. He was in two of my pictures and was the lead in one of Negri's silent movies.

"A realtor had taken over Valentino's former estate, Falcon's Lair. He allowed Pola Negri to live there and I took her up there the night she moved in. I am sure they had had a love affair. No question about that. She was in tears when I drove her up to Falcon's Lair. She'd point at the stables and say, 'There's where Rudy and I kept our horses.' Or when she went in the bedroom where she and Rudy slept, she cried all over the place."

Interestingly enough, I had spoken to director Billy Wilder during the course of interviewing Mr. Stone. He acknowledged that indeed he had considered Negri for the role of Norma Desmond in the 1950 blockbuster *Sunset Boulevard*. "Her accent worried me," he told me. He then approached America's Sweetheart, Mary Pickford, who refused the role. He chose Gloria Swanson after a friend suggested her. He was delighted with Swanson, and her performance earned her an Academy Award nomination.

Pola Negri

Hi Diddle Diddle's Adolphe Menjou and Pola Negri (RKO Radio, 1943).

The Secret of His Success

"I think directorial touches are a lot of crap. My specialty was making pictures on a 'no nonsense' basis with a crew of twenty and not two hundred as some of the pictures today. They have two or three hundred people on the crews today. My idea of size is about eight or nine people. It's crazy. It's insanity! I made *Confidence Girl* [1951] with a total crew of about twelve people."

Mr. Stone has sustained a career that lasted from silent films all the way into the early seventies. Few directors have this kind of longevity. What was the secret of his success?

"The fact I could make films of quality for less money than the others. And most of my jobs came because of my scripts. I never worked on *any* picture I didn't direct. And on practically all, I was the writer. I had more autonomy I think, over a longer period than anybody in the business because I could make films for less money. [Andrew Stone not only directed, he also produced and wrote the majority of his films. In later years, his former wife, Virginia, also produced films with him.]

"*Stormy Weather* [1943] was one of the few pictures I didn't produce. I directed it and I actually ended up writing the script but I didn't get credit, I just got directing credit."

Stormy Weather's **Bill Robinson, Lena Horne and Cab Calloway (20th Century-Fox, 1943).**

DIRECTORS, ACTORS AND CRITICS!

"I rate [Billy] Wilder as best director. Billy had a good story sense. As far as I can recall they were all entertaining pictures. On the other hand, I don't have much respect for William Wyler. I thought he was a lousy director in spite of all his Oscars. But that's just my opinion. He'd use twenty or thirty takes on everything.

"The greatest actress I ever worked with was Mae Marsh. She was one of the greatest actresses that ever *lived*. I used her in a couple of pictures. She was wonderful and a very nice woman. She was in *Birth of a Nation* [1915], the biggest part. She went into talking films in small parts. My favorite actor was James Mason. He was so professional and natural.

"The thing is, the critics are down on that type of musical. [Mr. Stone was referring to *Song of Norway* (1970) and *The Great Waltz* (1972).] You see, the critics want to be avant-garde. The critics are all getting on in age and they don't want the young people to think they're not with it, so they're all for avant-garde stuff.

"The musicals I was making at the end were *operettas*. *The Sound of Music* [1965] got *terrible* reviews and it was one of the biggest grossing pictures of all time! When I made *The Great Waltz*, I told Metro, 'We're going to get panned by the critics but the audiences will love it.' Besides, most of the critics don't know *anything* about music anyhow! So I expected it. I knew I'd get panned on *The Great Waltz*. *The Sound of Music* got worse reviews than I did.

"One critic from the *Hollywood Reporter* was such an ignoramus with musicals [that] he talked about Johann Strauss as a pianist! Of course he wasn't a pianist, he was a *violinist*. Everything he said in his review was completely wrong. He said there was original music in the picture. There wasn't *one note* that wasn't written by Johann Strauss! In Austria they gave great reviews to *The Great Waltz*. I told Metro, 'I don't care how good the picture is, we'll get lousy reviews because its an operetta and they think operettas are *passé*.'"

Working with Andy Stone

Actor Robert Stack and actress and opera singer Mary Costa talked about working with Andrew Stone. Stack had starred in *The Last Voyage* (1960), and Costa *The Great Waltz* (1972). Their admiration for him as director and friend was very evident.

The Last Voyage

"When you work with Andy and you work on location, boy, you better carry a lot of Blue Cross!" Robert Stack let out a long sigh and explained. "I must say we had a terribly exciting time doing that movie which should have been a *big smash* and was unfortunately misused by the then head of MGM. The fellow who was head of the studio had a picture that was in opposition to ours. He was also at that particular time a producer. A producer who became head of the studio! He had a movie called *Home from the Hill* [1960].

"Now instead of publicizing *all* of his products, he forgot our picture because his ego got in the way. He wanted his show to do better than any other show so he didn't do anything for ours, which would have been highly successful. But he publicized his *Home from the Hill* which fell on its ass and released ours in a blizzard in Texas!

"If you have no publicity and you have a bad release quotient, your movie's not going to go anywhere, no matter *how* good it is! When the studio is not behind you, you're in trouble. This was much more than a motion picture. This was an adventure!

"It was all done aboard ship in Japan and on the ocean itself. We almost got into a World War Three with Japan! The Japanese didn't want the ship sunk and they didn't want the engine room flooded, which is of course what Andy wanted—to show the ship sinking.

Stars of *The Last Voyage* (MGM, 1960), Dorothy Malone and Robert Stack.

"The Japanese may have agreed to a certain degree of destruction. How are you going to do it otherwise? But you're dealing with real stuff there so what happened was a very dangerous shoot and one guy almost had his head torn off!

"You're dealing with an old ship with years of grease and slime. They opened up the side of the ship and water came running in. We had fire boats out there pushing water through. I can remember Edmond O'Brien saying, 'God damn it! I'm not going to be a masochist and kill myself in this movie!'

"He said, 'We're all going to be electrocuted!' Well of course, they had live arcs and salt water and I got to tell you, it was a dangerous shoot. Instead of just doing sort of a studio arrangement, we had to wing it.

"The girl who played my daughter [Tammy Marihugh] kept calling me 'Mr. Stack.' I kept telling her to call me 'daddy' for the film. Well this went on for about ten days and then they had about a four by four strung across this blown-up hole which went down seventy feet! We were rigged on a small length of piano wire and no net as I remember. This little girl was just plain scared to death. So when she looked at me, she said, 'Daddy, daddy help me!' Boy, that wasn't acting. She was scared to death and so was I!

"I mean working over this hole; the explosions were real dynamite. It was real steel and it *wasn't* special effects. It was a very dangerous movie. I remember George Sanders cut an extra hole. He separated the two port holes so he could jump out in case the thing sank in the night! He's probably the only guy that would have gotten out!

"It was a dangerous, dangerous movie to make but Andy made it all work. All I can tell you, it was a king of shoot I wouldn't want to replicate—hauling Dorothy Malone up and down the stairs, oh man!

"But he's a great guy and he got screwed on that movie 'cause it was a damn good picture. He made do with what he had. I think of the average director with unlimited special effects, à la Spielberg, à la Zemeckis, having to go out there and just wing it, if you will.

"In the first place, a lot of actors wouldn't even do it. With real dynamite, real glass, holes seventy feet deep! Eddie O'Brien had very, very poor eyesight and he was afraid because he couldn't see. In other words, we were working under hazardous conditions the way they used to do it, maybe fifty or sixty years ago and Andy made it work.

"Andy had a terrible time with the tub boat operators who were in collusion and charged ten times as much once the ship was at sea. It was very tough. When you're out at sea, you can't 'throw a contract out the window.' This was very scary; some people were hurt. We had some underwater demolition teams who would do these really dangerous stunts. These guys were not stunt men, we're talking about the real Marines. One of the davits let go of a lifeboat and the guy fell about sixty feet!

"Andy's a neat guy. He's a throwback to the old days of picture making. He represents the golden age and that was an age when you made do. You just took the camera in the old days, over your shoulder. If there was sun on top of the hill, that's where you'd shoot. There was no time for ego or temperament. Your job was to make it work and he's an old timer. That's what his job was and he made it work! I had a wonderful time with him."

The Great Waltz

"My dream through my entire life was to make one really glamorous musical in the grand tradition of MGM." Soprano Mary Costa was already an established opera star when Andrew Stone expressed interest in her for his film *The Great Waltz* (1972). Shot on location in Vienna, Costa remembered her concerns during the film and how Mr. Stone's innate rapport with people taught her a wonderful lesson.

"The very first thing Mr. Stone was going to do was shoot a close-up on me. This big camera was really on top of me! On the stage, it is a long shot unless someone is watching you through opera glasses. I

The Great Waltz's **Mary Costa and Horst Bucholz (MGM, 1972).**

began arranging my face and twisting it all around, moistening my lips and everything. He was looking at me and I was a nervous wreck. He struck the set for another scene so he could take me into one of the anterooms and talk to me.

"It was the first shot and I was so mad at myself because I just could not relax. I shall never forget sitting in front of him knowing that I was going to get a reprimand because I was so nervous in front of the camera.

"He just smiled and said he'd been through this with all the great actresses with whom he had worked and that he knew how to straighten me out right away. I was not used to that old fashioned close-up camera which was practically on top of you. I had performed on television with the cameras behind the audience for *every* type of shot.

"First of all,' he said, 'if you think there's anything wrong with your face and you don't like it, forget it.' We're going to have a lot of close-ups in this picture and that's why I started with one of you first. You're going to *love* them before this picture is over but I realize you're accustomed to the space between the audience and the stage. But will you listen to what I have to say?'

The Great Victor Herbert stars Allan Jones and Mary Martin, 1939.

"And I said, 'Of course, with pleasure.' Then he said, 'But will you *really* listen?' I said, 'Yes, I will.' 'You *really* will?' he said again. 'Yes! I'm eager to know that answer!' 'Well,' he said smiling, 'you already do, it's *listening!* And you are only *now*, really listening to me.'

"He told me, 'When you truly listen, the face takes care of itself and you don't have to worry about expressions on your face. Your true thoughts do it for you. Don't *ever* let me see any blanks in your thought patterns because they register on your face. You certainly don't do this in your personal life and now your face must mirror your thoughts to *thousands* of people. Forget your looks! *Listen* and respond!'

"And after he had finished the alternate setup in the palace [filmed on location at the Schönbrunn Palace], he went back to the dining room scene and got my close-up on the first take! As I look back, it was one of my most memorable experiences. Someone on the crew complimented me on the close-up and I looked at Andrew Stone and he winked and smiled.

"That information carried over into my personal life and everything I did professionally. I realized that the art of listening keeps the

Rudolph Valentino

mind, your nerves and face, and your body intact. I've always been grateful to him for that terrific lesson.

"I have always thought about Andrew Stone, that he is a genius. He did what the famous conductor George Szell did, which was he taught with his heart and he felt with his mind. He is an elegant man with a great sense of humor."

CLOSING SEQUENCE

Andrew Stone continued: "I'm not interested in any recent films. I voted for *Il Postino* [*The Postman*—Italy, 1994]. I was a pioneer, that's true. I shot all on natural locations. I hadn't worked in a studio since around 1949. I never had an office in a studio. The office was right here in my home!"

I ask Mr. Stone how he'd like to be remembered. After all, his career has spanned decades and he remains a true Hollywood legend. He paused, then answered, chuckling softly, "I guess as a Maverick." He will also be remembered as a gentle and compassionate man. Thankfully he has left us a legacy of wonderful films.

......

FILMOGRAPHY

......

The Elegy—1926
Fantasy; Applejoy's Ghost—1927
Dreary House; Liebenstraum—1928
Adoration; Fantasy—1929
Sombras de Gloria (Blaze o' Glory)—1930
Hell's Headquarters—1932
The Girl Said No—1937
Stolen Heavey; Say It in French—1938
The Great Victor Herbert—1939
Hardboiled Canary (aka There's Magic in Music)—1941

Stormy Weather; Hi Diddle Diddle (aka Diamonds and Crime)—1943
Sensations of 1945—1944
Bedside Manner (aka Her Favorite Patient)—1945
The Bachelor's Daughter—1946
Fun on a Week-end, The Pretenders; Strange Bedfellows—1947
Highway 301—1950
Confidence Girl—1951
The Steel Trap—1952
Blueprint for Murder—1953
The Night Holds Terror—1955
Julie—1956

Cry Terror; The Decks Ran Red;
  Infamy at Sea—1958
The Last Voyage—1960
Ring of Fire—1961
The Password Is Courage—1962

Never Put It in Writing—1963
The Secret of My Success—1965
Song of Norway—1970
The Great Waltz—1972

Index